Prepared with the financial
assistance of UNESCO

Published simultaneously
in Great Britain
by Prentice-Hall International,
London

Administering
the Atom
for Peace

Administering the Atom for Peace *by J. E. Hodgetts*

Atherton Press
70 Fifth Avenue, New York
A Division of Prentice-Hall, Inc.
1964

ADMINISTERING THE ATOM FOR PEACE
J. E. Hodgetts

Copyright © 1964 by Prentice-Hall, Inc.
Atherton Press, New York, New York

Published simultaneously in Great Britain by
Prentice-Hall International, Inc.
28 Welbeck Street, London W.1, England

Atherton Press, A Division of Prentice-Hall, Inc.
70 Fifth Avenue, New York, New York, 10011

Library of Congress Catalog Card Number: 64-11506
Printed in the United States of America 00480

International Political Science Association Series

Administering the Atom for Peace
J. E. HODGETTS

Preface

The literature of public administration is deficient in comparative analyses. We shall probably have to wait for some years before a definitive treatise on comparative public administration can be written. Meanwhile, a logical and useful way to prepare the ground is to study specific problems. This study of the administrative problems associated with the peaceful applications of nuclear energy is presented as a modest contribution to this objective.

Comparative analyses are fraught with many perils, not the least of which is the temptation to seek administrative prescriptions that will be universally valid. Restraint should be exercised in accepting such formulas, for the factors that condition the practical application of policies vary enormously from one country to another. This note of caution having been sounded, it is nevertheless true that the administrative solutions to the problems posed by the emergent uses of atomic energy for peaceful purposes show a remarkable similarity despite the obvious differences in the formative institutional, economic, and technological features of each country. It is the purpose of this study to throw light on the impact of these shaping forces and on the particular administrative responses to them which have so many common elements. Hopefully, such a study will encourage more groups from the international community of social scientists to undertake similar inquiries into other specific areas. The construction of such building blocks may provide the foundation on which a more general treatise on comparative public administration can ultimately be erected.

The primary purpose of this study is to identify a number of problems commonly encountered by a representative sample of major countries having active programs for exploiting the peacetime potential of the atom. Sufficient historical and descriptive material has been included to familiarize the reader with the evolution of the organizational forms peculiar to each country in the survey. Factual detail has, however, been kept to the minimum essential to an understanding of the administrative solutions devised by each.

Although the present volume bears the name of only one author, it is actually the result of the combined effort of a number of people who, under the auspices of UNESCO and the International Political Science Association, were invited to prepare reports for their respective countries on this subject. These reports subsequently became the foundation for a series of discussions conducted as part of the program for the Fifth Triennial Congress of the International Political Science Association, which was held in Paris in September, 1961.

Altogether, six countries and a number of international authorities were selected as the subjects for separate reports. The sample is not very large, the selection being governed to some extent by the availability of interested scholars at the time the project was initiated and by the suggestion from UNESCO that certain countries be included. The major and most regrettable omission is a report on the situation in the Soviet Union. However, the three most prominent Western countries in the nuclear-energy field—the United States, the United Kingdom, and France —are represented; each has a joint program embracing military as well as civilian uses of atomic energy. Japan and Canada adequately typify the problems of medium-sized powers engaged solely in programs for the peaceful uses of nuclear energy. Italy, with perhaps the least specialized organization and least developed program, illustrates a possible departure from the norm set by the more advanced programs of the other countries in this survey. The inclusion of a descriptive analysis of the many international and regional organizations concerned with the supranational aspects of peaceful atomic-energy programs adds a dimension to the study and affords many striking parallels to the domestic organizations and problems examined in this survey.

It will be observed that, in presenting the material, the text departs from the usual international protocol of treating each country in alphabetical order. The order of presentation has been varied either to preserve a coherent chronological sequence in tracing a particular development or because the analysis of an organization or a procedure could best be carried out by grouping those countries which had demonstrably reacted in a similar fashion to the administrative problems with which they were confronted. The particular sequence employed here does not, then, reflect a ranking order deliberately based on particular assumptions about the nations' status as nuclear powers.

A special word of acknowledgment to and identification of the individual contributors to the symposium are in order because the somewhat unusual method of using and adapting their papers may create confusion about authorship and responsibility. The participating national reporters were J. E. Hodgetts, Canada, Hardy Professor of Political Science, Queen's University; Henri Puget, France, professor at the Institut d'Études Politiques de Paris, *conseiller d'état,* and director of the Centre de Droit de l'Énergie Atomique, Institut de Droit, University of Paris; Dr. Luigi Citarella, Italy, University of Rome and editor of *Diritto Ed Economia Nucleare;* Yoshio Kawashima, Japan, Atomic Energy Bureau, Science and Technics Agency; J. W. Grove, United Kingdom, senior lecturer, University of Manchester; Dr. Robert G. Cutler, United States, Office of Management and Organization, United States Bureau of the Budget; [1] Paul C. Szasz, International Atomic Energy Agency and related bodies, Legal Division, International Atomic Energy Agency. Professor Hodgetts served as *rapporteur général* for the sessions in Paris.

The material for this book has been largely taken from the working papers prepared by the above-named individuals and from the discussions which took place at the sessions in Paris.[2]

---

[1] We deeply regret having to report the untimely death of Dr. Cutler not long after making his contribution to this congress.

[2] Copies of the individual national reports are available in mimeographed form in French and English from the secretary general of the International Political Science Association, Paris.

The author, as *rapporteur général,* was invited by the joint sponsors of the project to prepare a study that would develop the findings and conclusions of the scholars involved. In this respect, the present study differs from an edited collection of papers prepared by each national reporter, the usual method of reporting the results of a symposium. The justification for adopting a different presentation is that it was believed that one author given a relatively free hand to work on the material *de novo* could produce a more succinct and genuinely comparative study through a careful synthesis of the material so generously placed at his disposal by the various participants. One important consequence of this decision is that the reader will find the text uses neither quotation marks nor footnotes as a means of ascribing particular statements or opinions to the individual national reporters. Only these people will be in a position to judge the extent to which the author has played the role of intellectual parasite in borrowing so heavily from their labors. Consciousness of this parasitism, it is hoped, has instilled a proper regard for an honest discharge of the responsibility conferred on the author to record data and comments with as little distortion as possible. It goes without saying that this book would have been impossible to prepare without the detailed research undertaken by others and their perceptive contributions to the round table held in Paris. That these people must henceforth remain anonymous should in no way induce the reader, any more than the author, to overlook the fact that the merits this volume may possess must be attributed to their efforts. By the same token, they must be absolved from any responsibility either for the mode of presentation or for whatever inaccuracies have unwittingly crept into this volume; for these, the author is obliged to take full responsibility.

A similar dispensation should be accorded UNESCO and the International Political Science Association, which initiated this inquiry by means of a contract and generously provided the financial sustenance required for the research.

Finally, the author records his personal thanks to his own university and to the Canada Council for making it possible to devote part of a sabbatical leave to the preparation of this study and to Nuffield College and its warden, D. Norman Chester, for providing such ideal conditions for undertaking the task.

J. E. Hodgetts

November 1963

Contents

List of Figures

I
Introduction

The past two decades have witnessed the introduction and exploitation of a new form of energy which, even as its destructive capacity casts a mushroom cloud of gloom over mankind, offers bright prospects for contributing to human well-being. Our concern here is entirely with the administrative problems associated with the peaceful applications of atomic energy. Nevertheless, what the psychologist might call the "ambivalence" of this energy source—equally and simultaneously capable of being put to destructive and constructive uses—has inescapable administrative consequences which will become clear.

The chain of events leading from the secluded retreats of the research physicist to the Manhattan Project and on to Hiroshima is too well known to bear repetition. Nor is the sad tale of frustrated and frustrating attempts to secure international control of the war-making capacities of the atom essential to this study other than to recognize that the current attempt to exploit the peaceful applications of nuclear energy are inseparably linked to the efforts to achieve international control of its military uses. These applications, the end products of a series of processes as extended and complex as the fission of the atom itself, also have a secondary place in this survey. The administrative problems of managing these various processes are the concern of this volume.

The end products in themselves are, of course, intensely interesting, but so much publicity has attended their introduction to the market that there is need for only the briefest comment at this point. The manifold peaceful uses of the atom fall into two broad categories: one, its use as a source of power and, two, its ability to create by-products in the form of radioactive isotopes with a seemingly inexhaustible array of practical applications.

In the simplest terms, power is derived from the heat which is released under controlled conditions in a nuclear reactor and is then conveyed to more conventional equipment for application to a variety of purposes. Chief among these and a matter of the most intensive current development is its conversion into electrical power as a supplement to and, in the future, a possible substitute for electricity developed by water resources or by such conventional fuels as coal and oil. Smaller, so-called packaged plants for providing heat and power to isolated communities—in the Arctic regions, for example—are also projected. Used as a means of propulsion, we have already progressed from Jules Verne's fantasy to the reality of the nuclear submarine; atom-powered surface vessels will follow and, in the future, aircraft and spaceships.

Within the reactor, either as a by-product of the fission that takes place or as a result of exposing certain elements to radiation, radioactive isotopes are also produced. These, in turn, are susceptible to an ever-expanding range of applications. In medicine they perform infinitely more refined therapeutic services than such forms of radiation as the X-ray tube. Irradiation and treatment of deep cancers or the injection of small quantities of irradiated material into diseased human tissue also open up new avenues for the treatment of disease. Similarly, for diagnostic and research purposes, tracer elements of irradiated material can be tracked through the human system. In agriculture the same procedure applied to the study of plant pathology or the determining of the value of fertilizers, for example, has experimental and practical applications which are being daily extended. Revolutionary changes in methods of processing and packing food products may be imminent as experiments with the effects of exposing such products to radiation proceed. The industrial uses of radioactive isotopes show equal promise. The tracer technique, through the use of radioactive gauges, solves many difficult problems in quality control, whether it be the determination of the density of tobacco in a cigarette or the uniform thickness of paper or the checking for flaws in a steel casting, leaks in an oil pipeline, wear in metal bearings or other, almost countless uses. Even the explosive power of the atom is being harnessed to such practical peacetime purposes as exploring for oil.

The euphoria engendered by the contemplation of man's ingenuity in harnessing the atom for his peacetime pursuits should not, however, distract us from a more mundane but equally necessary inquiry: has man been equally ingenious in devising administrative techniques to cope with the problems raised by the many peacetime applications of nuclear energy? Have engineers and scientists created problems that are beyond the administrative reach of the social engineer? Can we properly organize what we are called upon to administer? These are the questions to which the present study is directed in the hope that the experience of the several countries surveyed may provide some guidance in seeking the most appropriate administrative methods.

Superficially, the peacetime applications of atomic energy would appear to fall within the administrative competence of a single agency. In fact, this is not so; closer inspection reveals that such a variety of functions is involved that most countries have favored separate agencies to manage the several parts of the total program. For this reason and as a preliminary step in the analysis, the components need to be identified and the problems peculiar to each properly categorized. There are four major components worthy of separate consideration:

1. Provision of the nuclear material
2. Research and development
3. Commercial exploitation
4. Regulation and control

Interwoven with these four components are two more general considerations: (1) the international implications and (2) the problem of preserving accountability of the various agencies involved in each phase of administration. Co-ordination of the

work performed by specialized nuclear-energy agencies and relating their activities to the existing departments with which
they overlap will also be themes of this survey.

Provision of the Nuclear Material. The provision of nuclear
material relates to the preliminary exploration for the ore and
mining, extracting, refining, and marketing the material. If it
were not for the fact that nuclear material can be as readily deployed for warlike as for peaceful objectives, there would be
little reason to treat these operations in a way markedly different from the methods used for dealing with the production
of conventional minerals. Indeed, it is in this area that the existing methods of licensing and the prevailing relations between
the state and private enterprise have been least affected. Nevertheless, the provisions made by each nation for controlling the
various stages required for the production and distribution of
nuclear material demonstrate a universal concern for taking precautions which are not necessary for the production of other
minerals. These precautions range from complete state monopoly
over production and procurement to moderate control over the
distribution and use of all nuclear source material (as distinct
from the natural ore).

Obviously the key question here is: Assuming the need for
more than the usual degree of state control, to what extent
should the state itself participate in or even monopolize all the
preliminary activities necessary for the production of the final
source material? In Chapter IV this matter will be examined in
detail.

Research and Development. Two major features have characterized the activities listed under the heading "Research and
Development."

First, there has been a dramatic upsurge of activity following
the close of World War II, typified, for example, in the United
Kingdom by a growth in staff over a recent seven-year period
from 20,000 to 40,000 employees in the Atomic Energy Authority
or by the facts that in the French Atomic Energy Authority
(Commissariat à l'Énergie Atomique) the average age of the

employees is only thirty-three and in ten years the number of staff has increased about sixfold.

Second, accompanying this rapid rate of growth is what amounts to a unique telescoping of the usual time sequences in the research-developmental cycle. Normally, development occurs as an aftermath of research, sometimes with prolonged intervals between the findings of the research scientist and the development of applications. Particularly in the field of power-reactor technology, there is a new phenomenon in which all types of research and development are being conducted simultaneously with a feedback of experience in operation to the laboratories and engineering design rooms and revised designs, in turn, are being incorporated as construction of the new plant goes on.

Rapid expansion and the acceleration of the research-developmental cycle have a number of important consequences not only for the administrative organs of the state but also for the universities and industries associated with them in this phase of the atomic-energy program. Does the concentration of so many technical and scientific personnel in one field distort the over-all scientific program of the community by depriving other equally important areas of money, personnel, and equipment? To what extent should the state assume the traditional responsibilities of the universities for basic research and training? And, if the state does develop its own complex of scientific establishments on the gigantic scale demanded, what is the best way of organizing this massive apparatus and measuring the effectiveness of its performance? What should be the nature of industry's contribution, especially on the developmental side of the program?

These are a sample of the problems generated in all countries by the experience of the past two decades with the research and developmental components of a peacetime atomic-energy program. Needless to say, they are extended and aggravated in those countries which are also embarked on vast programs for military applications. The solutions, as noted in Chapter V, are conditioned by the state of each nation's industrial base, its experience with and training for research, and the stage of technological development attained in each case.

Commercial Exploitation. Reference has already been made to the varied end products emerging from the research on and development of nuclear energy. Clearly, the most important issues are raised in connection with the nuclear generation of power, more immediately for domestic and industrial purposes, but in the long run for the propulsion of craft under or on the seas or in the air. Once again, the issue is joined: How far or for how long should the state retain a hand in the commercial undertakings opened up by nuclear energy? What should be the nature of the partnership between the state and private enterprise if both are to share the obvious financial risks, as well as any long-run benefits, of this pioneering venture? The production, sale, and distribution of radioactive isotopes do not raise problems of the same magnitude; here it is largely a matter of regulating and possibly instructing the private firms or individuals who may be licensed to use the materials. Consideration of the practices that have developed in each of the countries in this survey is given in Chapter V as part of the analysis of the research and development problems.

Regulation and Control. It will be apparent that regulation of all the foregoing aspects of nuclear energy is inevitable. First, pending any satisfactory outcome to negotiations for adequate international control, the security of the state rests in the capacity of each nation to regulate the production of and commerce in the nuclear material itself. The hazards to the health and safety of those who work with the material and who are exposed to risks arising from the breakdown of reactors also demand regulation. A critical administrative issue raised specifically in the case of the United States is whether responsibility for these controls should be vested in the agency which is equally concerned with promotional and operational activities. This issue, among several others, is examined in Chapter VI.

Co-ordination. The organizational means of coping with the problems of regulation are particularly complicated by the fact that these problems may be a matter of concern not only to the agencies specifically involved in the administration of the peacetime uses of the atom but also to the departments regularly concerned with health, welfare, education, trade, and labor conditions in each nation. Another dimension of the problem of co-ordinating controls is added when, as is the case with two of the countries surveyed, both national and state or provincial agencies of government in a federally organized state have a joint interest in these matters. Co-ordination is discussed in Chapter VII.

The International Dimension. The peculiarly sensitive nature of nuclear energy has brought into being a variety of regional and international bodies generally combining both regulatory powers and operational or promotional responsibilities. The presence of these agencies makes necessary close collaboration with the national atomic-energy authorities of the member states while handling staff, budget, and co-ordination problems comparable in many ways with those faced by each nation. The relevant experience, practice, and problems at the international level will be incorporated in the succeeding chapters.

Accountability. The overriding need to preserve the traditional lay controls over both the operational and regulatory aspects of the nuclear-energy program appears as a universal and far-from-resolved issue in all countries. The impact of science on the policies of governments everywhere and the consequent influx of scientists and technicians into the public service raise anew the question of expert–layman relations which in the recent past were viewed largely as a problem in military–civil relations.

It is an interesting reflection of the social scientists' concern for such problems that the program of the Fifth Congress of the International Political Science Association included not only the specific case of nuclear energy but two other topics with broader ramifications—"Technocracy and the Role of Experts in Government" and "Civil–Military Relations in the Field of Foreign Policy-making." The rapid expansion of scientific and technical personnel, the largely untried character of the atomic-energy programs, and the hazardous nature of the substances and processes employed have forced dependence on the judgment of the scientist, both as administrator and policy-maker, that arouses concern for the maintenance of the traditional lay controls of the political executive and a representative legislature. In this respect, atomic energy provides an outstanding illustration of the adjustments that may have to be made in order to absorb the scientist into the existing governmental framework. Comment on this general issue is in the final chapter of this book.

Even this preliminary sketch of the peacetime administration of atomic energy should be sufficient to reveal the many-sided character of the problems confronting each nation and the international community in their endeavors to exploit the full peacetime potential of nuclear energy. In the following chapters these interlocking, though separable, elements of the program will be examined, demonstrating the administrative response of the countries surveyed to the complex issues outlined here.

II
The Need for Special
Atomic-Energy Authorities

The experience of all the countries in this survey confirms the judgment that administrative problems associated with the peaceful uses of atomic energy are of such special character that they cannot be effectively handled by any of the existing administrative agencies. In fact, the complexities of the vast enterprises devoted to promoting and controlling the nuclear-energy program have induced some countries to create more than one organization for dealing with the various problems.

The preference for specialized atomic-energy agencies can best be explained by examining their evolution in each country as well as noting the similar lines of development at the international level.

The United States. Despite the early discovery of the phenomenon of radioactivity, to which scientists had been attracted since 1896, it was not until 1939 that the possibility of releasing through fission large amounts of energy for military or other purposes became known. Even then, it is interesting to observe that American-born scientists were so unaccustomed to the idea of using their research for military purposes that the early efforts to obtain government support "were stimulated largely by a small group of foreign-born physicists." [1]

---

[1] H. D. Smyth, *A General Account of the Development of Methods of Using Atomic Energy for Military Purposes under the Auspices of the United States Government, 1940–45* (Washington, D.C.: Government Printing Office, 1945), p. 26.

9

The first governmental initiative was taken by Pres. Frank-
lin D. Roosevelt when, in 1939, he appointed a committee to
look into the matter. The committee was impressed by the possibilities of nuclear energy not only for atomic weapons but also
as a source of power. During World War II these flirtations with
the atom eventuated in the establishment of the Manhattan Engineering District, a special organization under the Corps of Engineers in the then Department of War, created specifically for
the purpose of directing engineering and procurement aspects
of the program that would eventually produce the first atom
bomb. By 1943 the Manhattan Project was co-ordinating the
total atomic-energy efforts of the nation, operating with appropriations that were hidden in other accounts in order to conceal
the real nature and extent of the project.

Immediately after the war, while the military potential of
atomic energy was still very much in the fore, public opinion
generally supported a proposal to vest in the state complete
powers for controlling and developing the use of this new form
of energy. Two central questions then had to be resolved by the
Senate Committee on Atomic Energy, which was set up to consider the legislation: (1) Was a special atomic-energy agency
necessary?; (2) Should the program be placed in military or
civilian hands?

The strongest official opposition to the proposed specialized
agency came from Secretary of State Harold Ickes. Testifying before the Senate committee, he argued:

> Atomic fission is too big a matter to be set off in a field by itself
> with a fence around it and separated from the problems with
> which the regular departments of the Government have to deal.
> Atomic energy is part of the larger problem of energy. . . . in
> the space of our national existence the jump from man power and
> animal power to electricity in the field of production, communica-
> tion and transportation was wholly revolutionary. Yet we did
> not find it necessary to set up a Federal department of steam or
> electricity or to alter the essential form of our Government to
> meet the problems thus created. . . . I content myself with saying
> that if the existing governmental departments that are properly
> concerned with international relations, military defense, national
> resources, power and technology are not qualified to carry on
> with an atomic age they ought to be abolished; otherwise they

ought to participate, within their appropriate fields, in the control of atomic energy.

The opposing opinion expressed by many experts was "that the development of atomic energy for the peaceful pursuits of mankind and for military purposes . . . should be directed and controlled by the Federal Government through a single permanent commission whose members . . . should be wholly devoted to that single duty and no other." [2] It was this position that prevailed, resulting in the creation of the Atomic Energy Commission by the Atomic Energy Act of 1946. Indeed, in the declaration of policy contained in the act, the legislators went out of their way to stress the unique qualities of atomic energy which had induced them to approve the legislation:

> The significance of the atomic bomb for military purposes is evident. The effect of the use of atomic energy for civilian purposes upon the social, economic, and political structures of today cannot be determined. . . .
> It is reasonable to anticipate, however, that tapping this new source of energy will cause profound changes in our present way of life. Accordingly, it is hereby declared to be the policy of the people of the United States that, subject at all times to the paramount objective of assuring the common defense and security, the development and utilization of atomic energy shall, so far as practicable, be directed toward improving the public welfare, increasing the standard of living, strengthening free competition in private enterprise, and promoting world peace.[3]

Having established that a special atomic-energy agency was necessary, there remained the question of civilian versus military control. In the formal sense this question was resolved in favor of civilian control by conferring ultimate power over the agency on the president. He annually establishes the amount of fissionable material to be produced, and the commission can engage in the production of atomic weapons or weapons parts only to the extent that the president's express consent and direction have been obtained. Further strengthening of civilian control is provided by the Joint Congressional Committee on Atomic Energy which is unique in the American system of government.

---

[2] Special Committee on Atomic Energy, *Atomic Energy Act of 1946*, S. Rep. No. 1211, 79th Cong., 2nd Sess. (1946), p. 47.

[3] Pub. L. No. 585, 79th Cong., 2nd Sess. (1946).

Recognition of the overriding requirements of national security meant, however, that the new commission could not be given exclusive jurisdiction over atomic energy. In its military applications, as the Senate committee made clear, "wherever these areas are involved, provision is made for full military participation, and independent activities of the military departments, especially in research and development, are not infringed but expressly encouraged." [4]

During the first five or six years of its existence, the Atomic Energy Commission directed most of its attention to the problems of developing, testing, and producing nuclear weapons and, to a more limited extent, developing reactors for the propulsion of submarines. In conjunction with these activities, extensive laboratory and production facilities were built and operated under the aegis of the commission. When, in the mid-1950's, it became clear that the civilian uses of atomic energy showed great promise, the Atomic Energy Act of 1946 was amended. The amended Act of 1954 left the original organizational arrangements virtually unchanged, but the commission was now expected to contract out much of its work to universities and industry and generally to foster greater collaboration in the whole program by the private sector. Although this partial transfer of operational and promotional activities to non-governmental agencies lightened the managerial tasks of the commission, at the same time it created regulatory problems of much greater scope and complexity.

As a result, the present organization for administering the peaceful uses of atomic energy in the United States bears the imprint of the original and primary concern for the war-making potential of the atom. This combination of purposes in a single agency is perhaps the most striking administrative feature of the atomic-energy program and helps explain the need for a separate, specialized agency. The experience and practice of other countries, even when the program is entirely devoted to peaceful applications, are also influenced by the dominant military implications of the atom.

---

[4] Special Committee on Atomic Energy, *op. cit.*, pp. 11–12.

The United Kingdom. The experience of the United Kingdom in the formative stages of its atomic-energy program parallels that of the United States. The experimental and theoretical work of such pioneer physicists as Lord Rutherford and Prof. P. M. S. Blackett came to a head in 1941 with Sir Winston Churchill's directive: "Although I am personally quite content with existing explosives, I feel we must not stand in the path of improvement." [5] Since British resources were fully absorbed in the war, the task of realizing the practical explosive potential of the atom was undertaken in the United States on the basis of a co-operative agreement emerging from the Quebec Conference in August, 1943. The secret directorate, sheltered in the Department of Scientific and Industrial Research under the innocent title of "Tube Alloys," was transferred almost intact to the Los Alamos station in California; a joint Canadian–British project, under the direction of Dr. Hans Halban and later Sir John Cockcroft, initiated the venture that culminated in the ZEEP research pile at Chalk River, Ontario.

The decision to maintain this collaborative arrangement for the duration of the war effectively broke off Britain's atomic-energy program and made it necessary to start anew at the close of hostilities. In any event, the withdrawal of British scientists from the United States was accompanied by the passing of the Atomic Energy Act in that country, which imposed such rigorous security restrictions on the exchange of atomic information that the United Kingdom was forced to take an independent path. That path, however, was strewn with the same hazards as those confronting the United States: the peaceful applications of atomic energy were still unknown, and military considerations dominated the research and developmental aspects of the program. Moreover, as a white paper, *The Future Organization of the United Kingdom Atomic Energy Project,* commented in 1953:

> [L]arge industrial concerns . . . which might, in other circumstances, have been willing and able to undertake major tasks in the field of atomic energy [would find] their resources fully com-

---

[5] Central Office of Information, *Nuclear Energy in Britain* ("Reference Pamphlets," No. 28 [3rd ed.; London: Her Majesty's Stationery Office, 1962]), p. 5.

mitted to the task of reconversion to peace-time production in
order to meet the overriding needs for the rebuilding of our
exports. . . .[6]

The white paper concluded, "only a Government-sponsored organization could provide the financial and other resources needed
for the novel, complicated and costly establishments which research and development would require." [7] In these circumstances,
it was not open to the British government to develop a program
which involved, in the initial stages at least, a heavy reliance on
the resources of universities and private contractors.

Assuming that the main burden of the atomic-energy program would fall on the state, the question of the most desirable
form of administrative machinery immediately arose. During the
war, the Department of Scientific and Industrial Research had
been responsible for the military aspects of atomic energy; enlarged by the addition of a program for peaceful applications,
the entire program was later transferred to one of the existing
departments, the Ministry of Supply. As Britain's defense procurement department, the ministry appeared to be most ad-
vantageously placed to assume the burden of a program which
would be militarily oriented for some time to come. Also, it
had at its disposal many surplus war facilities and a staff that
had the required practical experience of large-scale industrial
organization and that was being freed for other assignments.

In November, 1946, assent was given to the Atomic Energy
Act, which embodied the decision to transfer from the Department of Scientific and Industrial Research to the Ministry of
Supply responsibility for the atomic-energy program. An Atomic
Energy Research Establishment was set up at Harwell, Berkshire,
and a dozen men, only one of whom had any knowledge of atomic
energy, formed the nucleus of a production division which, in
the next twelve years, was to swell to a staff of over 17,000 people.

Intense activity under the auspices of these agencies placed
Britain in a position to explode a nuclear device in 1952 and
with that to turn more of its resources toward a program for the

---

[6] United Kingdom House of Commons, *The Future Organization of the
United Kingdom Atomic Energy Project,* Cmd. 8986 (1953), paragraphs 4–5.
[7] *Loc. cit.*

peaceful uses of atomic energy. By this time, the Ministry of Supply, in addition to its other responsibilities, was confronted in the atomic-energy field alone with the task of supervising industrial and research establishments that employed nearly 20,-000 people and had assets of £150,000,000 in plants and equipment. Clearly, a fresh look at the organization was required, particularly if the atomic-energy program was to be oriented to the peacetime applications.

The resultant official position was declared in 1953:

> As the industrial uses of atomic energy become relatively more prominent, the case for a form of control of the project which is more akin to the structure of a big industrial organization than to that of a Government department becomes increasingly strong; and it will, in the Government's view, become stronger with the increase in the need for closer contact and co-operation with industry, including the nationalized industries, and the widening application of atomic techniques.

"It is considerations such as these," the white paper continued, "which have led the Government to conclude that the most rapid and economical development in this field will be secured by transferring responsibility from the Ministry of Supply to a non-Departmental organization. . . ." A public corporation "run on industrial lines and with no responsibility outside the field of atomic energy" was the organizational prescription.[8]

In 1954, the United Kingdom Atomic Energy Authority was created to implement this proposal. The authority was empowered to take over not only all peaceful research and development, but also to conduct the necessary military research. The latter function, along with the supply of fissile material for atomic devices, was to be performed, however, on an agency basis for the Ministry of Supply (later for the Ministry of Aviation), which retained responsibility for the procurement of conventional components.

Once again, as in the United States, the activities associated with the war-making potential of nuclear energy had to be carried forward into the organization also directed to the peaceful applications. Moreover, because of the slow start on the program

---

[8] Paragraphs 11–12.

in the United Kingdom, the government was required to play a much more positive role in the development of the atomic programs than did the government of the United States. In fact, to anticipate, it is clear that a similar conclusion emerges from an examination of the experience of all the other countries included in this survey: despite the collaboration between the state and various private parties that has recently grown up in each of these countries, the arrangements in the United States show a more marked participation by the private sector.

Canada. Canada's initial involvement in the field of atomic energy came as a result of the agreement on collaboration between the United States and the United Kingdom at the Quebec Conference. As in the United States and the United Kingdom, Canada began its atomic-energy program in the hothouse atmosphere of war, and the program still bears the marks of the secrecy and fear generated by the awesome war-making potential locked in the atom. In conjunction with Britain, Canada pioneered the development of an experimental reactor capable of producing plutonium, a material which does not occur in nature but is a vital ingredient for the manufacture of nuclear bombs. From this modest joint undertaking has burgeoned an extensive, independent research and developmental program directed solely to the peaceful applications of this new and versatile source of energy.

In addition, Canadian developments have been affected by Canada's position as one of the major producers of uranium ore and concentrates, which constitute the raw material for all nuclear-energy activities.

Until the close of the war, it was possible to administer the scientific and developmental aspects of the program through a special establishment, physically separated from the headquarters of its parent, the National Research Council, but formally regarded as only one of the many divisions under that agency. The special position of Canada as a source of supply for the primary raw materials necessitated the early formation of a Crown company, Eldorado Mining and Refining Ltd., which, for three years after its creation in 1944, was given a complete monopoly of all stages of production and supply of uranium. Although private mining interests were subsequently permitted to explore for and extract the uranium ore, the Canadian government continues to monopolize the refining of the ore and nearly all the supply of the metal.

As in other countries, the peacetime possibilities of atomic energy necessitated a re-examination of the *ad hoc* arrangements which had been satisfactory for the wartime program but were being stretched beyond their capacities at the close of the war. In addition to the agency created to supervise the source material, Canada proceeded to establish two new agencies. The first of these, the Atomic Energy Control Board, was set up in 1946 and given comprehensive statutory powers over research, utilization of atomic energy, acquisition of mines and substances, and, generally, regulation of all health aspects of the atomic-energy program. In practice, the board assumed no operating role and, even for the regulatory aspects of its work, has tended to rely on other agencies. The second new body was set up in 1952 to take over from the National Research Council the wartime research and development establishment at Chalk River. The rapid build-up of staff and plant to explore the peaceful applications of the atom now clearly warranted a special agency unless the Research Council was to be swallowed by one of its offspring.

The result of these developments in Canada is that not one, but three, specialized agencies have been created to preside over the varied operations and to devise the regulations for the atomic-energy program. The gradual involvement of private enterprise —first in the production of source material, later in the research and developmental cycle, and most recently in the commercial exploitation of nuclear power—still leaves the state and its special agencies in a position of pre-eminence.

France. Initiation of an atomic-energy program in France was delayed, even more than in Britain, by the war and by immediate postwar conditions. France's wartime contribution was made by a handful of scientists who collaborated with the allies in the United States and Canada. The Occupation prevented any domestic build-up of the scientific personnel and establishments required for the exploration and exploitation of atomic-energy.

At the close of the war, the French economy was at a low ebb, there were no stocks of uranium, France was not a party to the "secret" of the bomb, and the tight security restrictions (even among the allies themselves) combined to place the nation at a great disadvantage.

Despite these unpromising circumstances, France could not afford to play the role of a spectator. In 1945, on the initiative of the minister of reconstruction, the provisional government approved an ordinance which provided for the creation of the Atomic Energy Authority (Commissariat à l'Énergie Atomique). The new agency was responsible for conducting all research and development in the utilization of atomic energy for scientific, industrial, and defense purposes. However, the late entry of France into the field tended to reverse the process experienced by the early starters, who had to graft the emergent peacetime activities on to a program oriented almost exclusively to war-making. France, on the other hand, started with no administrative commitments and was free to concentrate immediately on the peaceful uses of atomic energy. Indeed, the initial lack of raw materials, scientific knowledge, and staff left the country with no other option; it was a question of building from the ground up with the ultimate objective of preparing the way for France's entry into the "nuclear club."

Under the spirited direction of the authority, the complex skeleton of a vast technical and scientific structure was built with remarkable speed. Within a few years this structure proved capable of sustaining a program directed to military purposes as well. On February 13, 1960, France became the fourth country to explode a nuclear bomb and since then, like the other members of the nuclear club, has devoted the lion's share of the atomic-energy budget to research and development on military applications of nuclear energy.

In France's postwar condition, a new venture of such costly dimensions and national significance could be initiated and operated only by the state. The direct operating responsibilities of the Atomic Energy Authority necessitated the creation of a huge complex of government-owned mines, mills, and refineries, as well as state-run research and development establishments.

From about 1957, however, the pattern of collaboration between the state and various interested sectors of private industry and the universities began to emerge in much the same fashion as in the other countries already considered. The state's share in this program and its full responsibility for controlling all developments are still pre-eminent, and for most of these tasks the specialized public body, the Atomic Energy Authority (under the guidance of a board presided over by the prime minister or his delegate), is the primary agency.

Japan. As the only country to have suffered from direct exposure to the atom bomb, Japan had the most urgent incentive to direct its atomic-energy program solely to peaceful, civilian applications. This war-engendered attitude received a more positive impetus in the mid-1950's, as the peacetime potential of nuclear energy became increasingly apparent. The practical outcome was that three parties in the Japanese Diet jointly sponsored a measure to provide the finances for the initial steps in developing a peaceful program. As in France, this entailed a completely fresh start, for under the Occupation policy even scientific study of the atom was suspended until 1947. In 1954, after the approval of the first appropriation bill for an atomic-energy program, a high-level policy committee, the Preliminary Research Committee for the Use of Atomic Energy, was formed. Its inquiries were aided by the Japan Science Council, a government organization that conveyed the views of the scientific community to the prime minister. Further preliminary evaluation was undertaken by a mission that was sent abroad at the end of 1954, and the first United Nations International Conference on Atomic Energy, held in August, 1955, contributed still more information. In November of that year, the first Japanese–United States agreement on civilian uses of atomic energy was signed. The culmination of these studies and agreements was the unanimous approval by the Diet in December, 1955, of the Atomic Energy Basic Act.

This act laid down the principles which were to guide those concerned with developing the atomic-energy program as well as the general administrative framework within which the prin-

ciples could be implemented. Separate enactments provided successively for an Atomic Energy Commission to advise the prime
minister; an Atomic Energy Bureau, at first in the Prime Minister's Office, but transferred in 1956 to a newly created co-ordinating agency for science, the Science and Technics Agency; the
Japan Atomic Energy Research Institute; and the Atomic Fuel
Corporation.

The explanation for this seeming abundance of administrative agencies each directed exclusively to one activity is to
be found in one of the guiding principles enunciated in the
Atomic Energy Basic Act: research on and the use of atomic
energy were to be undertaken, as much as possible, with local
resources and minimum reliance on imported technology. This
policy directive ran counter to the past sixty years' experience,
during which Japan had relied heavily on imported technology
to support its industrial base. For its success, the new policy
clearly had to rely on direct state involvement in all aspects
of the nuclear-energy program. Even more than in Canada, this
has resulted in a proliferation of state agencies each sharing part
of the responsibility for meeting the varied objectives comprehended in the total program. As with the other countries under
review, the collaboration of universities and private enterprises
has been sought, but, not unexpectedly, the state's agencies continue to dominate the field.

Italy. In the last of the six countries covered in this survey,
the organization and program for nuclear energy are somewhat
less developed. Over the past several years a series of draft bills
has sought to provide a statutory foundation for the program and
a permanent organization to co-ordinate it. Thus far none of the
measures has been fully approved, with the result that Italy still
lacks an organic nuclear law.[9] By a curious reversal of traditional
legal evolution, this gap has been filled to some extent by rely-

---

[9] At the time of writing, the legislature was considering a much amended
draft of a portion of Part II of the bill generally known as the Colombo bill,
which was passed in emasculated form in 1960. In December, 1962, this
amended draft bill was approved. (See *Gazetta Ufficiale della Republica
Italiana,* No. 27, pp. 493–498.)

ing on the rules promulgated by an international organization, the European Community for Atomic Energy, to which Italy, as a member, adheres. As a result, international rules have been incorporated in the municipal law in default of any domestic legislation to cover the subject.

Prior to 1953, the only organization with a direct interest in nuclear energy was the Studies and Experience Information Center (Centro Informazioni Studi Esperienze), set up in 1946 on the initiative of a few industries and scientists in Milan. The center, which was designed to foster research in the industrial uses of atomic energy, subsequently became a company under the mixed ownership of private enterprises and several public authorities.

By 1953, mounting interest in the new source of energy and the necessity of developing international contacts with countries already possessing specialized atomic-energy organizations induced the Italian government to establish an *ad hoc* National Committee for Nuclear Research (Comitato Nazionale per le Ricerche Nucleari). The committee was given broad responsibilities over the whole atomic-energy field and was empowered to conduct its own research or sponsor and co-ordinate the work of other agencies and to serve as a center for fostering international co-operation. Hampered at the outset by a lack of funds of its own and by the failure to give it a legal personality, the committee had no genuinely independent status and had to rely on securing money and co-operation from other agencies.

In 1956, the committee produced a five-year plan for the future development of nuclear energy in Italy and at the same time received some independent funds. In addition, a National Institute for Nuclear Physics, created by amalgamating the relevant scientific work being undertaken at several university physics institutes, was placed at the disposal of the committee.

This modest strengthening of the organizational base did not go far enough, and, in 1960, after a number of conferences over draft bills, a somewhat emasculated "shortened" Italian nuclear law was enacted. Although the law for the first time gave a firmer statutory form to the Committee for Nuclear Energy by converting it into a public board, it was clear that the period

of indecision and of *ad hoc* solutions had left the committee to
face an uphill battle to claim the powers proper to its new status.
In effect, existing departments had already carved out from the
total atomic-energy field that portion which was relevant to their
own major concerns. The committee appears, therefore, to be
left with a residue of regulatory and operational tasks associated
with research on and development of atomic energy. Even these,
particularly as they relate to nuclear power developments, are
under the closest supervision of the Ministry of Industry and
Commerce. Of the countries under study, Italy appears to have
made the least use of administrative organs especially devoted
to the various aspects of a program for the peaceful uses of atomic
energy. This may reflect the somewhat less sophisticated state of
development in that country, but on present evidence, even with
an expanded program, it would appear that existing departments have been able to assert and consolidate an entrenched
interest in administering the separate portions of the program.

The Regional and International Level. The rapid development of special administrative organs for dealing with the peaceful uses of nuclear energy in each nation has been paralleled by
a similar proliferation of regional and international organizations
devoted to the same objectives. Indeed, the first resolution passed
by the General Assembly of the United Nations in 1946 called
for the establishment of a United Nations Commission on Atomic
Energy. Significantly, its terms of reference and early actions, as
was true of similar national bodies, reflected the preoccupation
with the military character of the new source of energy. The ambitious, but, unfortunately, ill-fated, plan to create an international body with exclusive jurisdiction over all intrinsically dangerous operations in the field of nuclear energy, coupled with
regulatory powers over national and private undertakings for its
peaceful application, foundered in the Cold War atmosphere.
Intense national preoccupation with rapid exploitation of the
military potential of the atom, the effort to hug the secret close
to each nation's bosom, and the Soviet Union's success in mas-
tering the mystery of the atom bomb brought all efforts at international collaboration to a standstill in the late 1940's.

During the next decade, however, an almost bewildering assortment of international and regional organizations began to appear. Thus, in 1950–1951, Norway and Holland joined forces to form the Joint Establishment for Nuclear Research for the purpose of operating an experimental reactor. On the initiative of UNESCO, expert studies and conferences led to the creation in 1954 of a permanent European Council for Nuclear Research (CERN). In 1956, a parallel agency, the Joint Institute for Nuclear Research (JINR), was set up by countries of eastern Europe and northern Asia.

These joint efforts to sponsor basic research were matched in the mid-1950's by the formation of a number of international and regional organizations directed to the developmental aspects of nuclear energy. In 1954, the national atomic-energy authorities of twelve European countries formed the European Atomic Energy Society to encourage co-operative research in peaceful applications of nuclear energy. The same year saw the establishment by the General Assembly of the United Nations of an Advisory Committee on Peaceful Uses of Atomic Energy. The great assemblage of scientists that convened in Geneva two years later at the instigation of the Advisory Committee made it clear that scientific developments in all parts of the world were proceeding on such similar lines that it was both useless and economically wasteful to continue the current policies of complete national self-sufficiency. In 1957, the six members of the Coal and Steel Community signed two treaties in Rome, one providing for the Common Market and the other for co-operation in atomic energy (the European Atomic Energy Community [EURATOM]). The Council of the Organization for European Economic Cooperation similarly established a European Nuclear Energy Agency which, in turn, gave rise to a series of conventions for a variety of collaborative projects for the peaceful uses of atomic energy. And, in the same period, after several years' negotiation, a statute for the creation of the International Atomic Energy Agency was signed by eighty nations, ratified, and entered into force on July 29, 1957. Subsequently there have been other agencies—for example, in 1959 the Inter-American Nuclear Energy Commission, an adjunct to the Organization of

American States—and an extension of joint research programs under the sponsorship of these regional and international bodies.

Conclusions. This brief account of the evolution of the organizational means of dealing with the peaceful applications of atomic energy helps answer the question with which this chapter began: Is atomic energy so unique that a program for its development cannot be contained by the existing governmental portfolios, thus necessitating the creation of one or more agencies devoted solely to atomic energy? The evidence, both with respect to each country and in the international sphere, strongly reinforces the claim for specialized atomic-energy authorities.

The primary reason has been emphasized: the ambivalence of nuclear energy—which is equally capable of warlike and peaceful applications—has induced all countries to view nuclear energy with a unique mixture of trepidation and anticipation. As has been noted, the special conditions of security and secrecy attending the initial wartime applications of atomic energy early set the stage for treating it as something apart from an ordinary operation. The growing attention to peacetime applications has never altered this unusual feature, for security still remains a matter of major national concern as long as international control of nuclear military devices continues to be frustrated. The security precautions which were imperative in war have been brought forward to the uneasy peacetime period, and the necessity for state control has been accentuated because of the failure to achieve international control. Similarly, the coming of peace and the emphasis on peaceful applications have not changed the intrinsic hazards to health which the explosion of the atomic bomb so dramatically portrayed. Indeed, it may be that the psychological impact of the awesome destructive power of the atom has induced all nations to develop exaggerated notions of the special provisions required for reassuring their people that all is well.

There were other practical considerations which impelled all nations, singly and in collaboration, to create special administrative devices for handling the peaceful applications of nuclear energy. It was clear that, in order to mount an effective program, enormous financial and scientific resources would be required. Even in a country as wealthy and as technically advanced as the United States, it was realized that, if the new programs were to be grafted to the conventional programs of existing departments or agencies, they would be thrown out of balance or even swallowed by the gargantuan requirements of the newcomer. For example, the dimensions of the atomic-energy effort may be seen in their true proportion if we note that in both Canada and in Japan, which have only peaceful atomic-energy programs, current allocations represent approximately one-quarter of each nation's total budget for scientific and developmental purposes. In countries like the United States, France, and Britain, where military applications still absorb the larger portion of the budget for atomic-energy development, the impact on the over-all national scientific effort is even greater.

The very dimensions of the program provided additional support, certainly at the initial stages of development, for setting up specialized agencies that would formally acknowledge the status and political importance of this new field of scientific endeavor. This consideration was particularly relevant in countries like Britain or France which, even though scientifically advanced, got a slow postwar start in the atomic-energy race and needed to close the gap as rapidly as possible. For a country like Japan, historically dependent on imported technology and yet dedicated to becoming nationally self-sufficient in the emergent field of nuclear energy, the need for a special group of agencies to mobilize the finances and concentrate the scarce scientific resources and manpower required was even more imperative. In all countries this hasty build-up could best be achieved by means of a co-ordinated effort on the part of state agencies specifically dedicated to this objective.

Another practical problem, perhaps most peculiarly present in countries like Japan and Italy, was that the rapid growth of international commitments and organizations, either regional or broader in scope, made it imperative for the countries to create special domestic agencies of their own to provide the necessary liaison. Indeed at the supranational level, specialized authorities to promote basic research and the peaceful application of nuclear energy were brought into being substantially in response to the same pressures that produced similarly specialized national organs. The dominance of military aspects of nuclear energy gave rise to the hope that an international body, such as the International Atomic Energy Agency, could become an instrument for neutralizing the war-making potential of the atom by inducing major nuclear powers to make significant quantities of fissionable materials available to the agency for peaceful purposes and thereby equitably reduce their war-making capacity. In fact, both this body and other regional organizations like EURATOM have received authority to supervise member states only to prevent the diversion to warlike purposes of materials and efforts destined for peaceful purposes. Member states of EURATOM, for example, still maintain complete control over activities declared to be military, and the International Atomic Energy Agency is limited to activities which member states have voluntarily submitted to its control. This situation is an international parallel to the pattern evolved in most member nations whereby the domestic atomic-energy authority acts on an agency basis to meet the requirements of the military establishments or else shares administration of the program with them.

The costliness of atomic-energy programs, which necessitated the co-ordination of effort in special national agencies, has had similar consequences at the international level. The high costs of reactors, chemical or isotope separation plants, and high-energy accelerators have encouraged international, regional or bilateral pooling arrangements. In programs which have developed along similar lines, it is clearly wasteful not to take advantage of various means of collaborating across national frontiers on research, exchange of information, and joint investment in and operation of elaborate and costly facilities. Moreover, for the economically and technologically underdeveloped nations, these organizations provide the only sensible method of entering the atomic-energy field.

The health hazards and safety problems associated with national atomic-energy programs also have international dimensions which suggest the need for specialized regulatory bodies vested with supranational authority. Pollution of international waters or of the atmosphere because of waste disposal or accidents are the most obvious illustrations. Growing international trade in nuclear and radioactive materials and conventions dealing with insurance and liability problems, regulation of transportation, packaging, and labeling similarly demand action by organizations that transcend national boundaries. The fact that for all countries nuclear-energy programs are a matter of direct concern to state instrumentalities also necessitates the formation of international bodies to foster transactions which are essentially intergovernmental and not altogether part of normal trading relations.

It is therefore apparent that there are as many unique international problems as there are unique domestic problems and that in each area the need for specialized atomic-energy agencies has made itself felt. Just as no nation could incorporate these new programs into any of its existing administrative bodies, so no obvious existing agency was capable of assuming international jurisdiction. Indeed, when the United Nations Charter was signed, the first bomb had not yet been exploded. Even had the need been foreseen, none of the existing organs of the United Nations possessed the managerial, proprietary, inspecting or licensing powers necessary to effect international control and development of nuclear energy. If the program had been incorporated into one of the existing agencies, it would have had the same consequences which induced each member nation to steer away from this solution: it was of such dimensions that it would have distorted the programs and budgets of any of the specialized international agencies to which it might have been attached.

In summary, the almost explosive development of nuclear-energy programs for both warlike and peaceful purposes, accompanied by problems of regulating and controlling the security and health hazards implicit in exploiting the atom, has fostered the creation of highly specialized organs to administer these programs in each nation and among nations. There can be no doubt that, after the first two decades of frenzied development, nourished as it was by war and Cold War conditions, the active participation of the state in all aspects of the program has been most pronounced. It is clear that the peculiar attributes of the atom, not the least of which is its simultaneous application to peaceful and warlike pursuits, will necessitate the continuation of more than the usual amount of state intervention.

III
Organizing a
Peaceful Atomic-Energy Program

For both domestic and international purposes, most countries have concluded that an effective nuclear-energy program can be launched only by separating it from other fields and forming special administrative organs for it. In the previous chapter the reasons for giving nuclear-energy development such special attention were evaluated; it is now appropriate to examine the organizational forms which have been devised by each country to meet the administrative challenge of applying the atom to peaceful purposes.

Three of the countries covered in this survey have simultaneously mounted programs for the military as well as the peaceful applications of nuclear energy. Consequently, the atomic-energy organizations in the United States, Britain, and France actually embrace dual responsibilities the fulfillment of which involves much interlocking of activities and close association with the armed services. Because the warlike applications of nuclear energy are not considered here, the organization in the armed services and the parts of the civil organization which work with them on such matters as weapon-testing will form no part of the following descriptive material.

The nuclear-energy program of each country comprehends many separate activities related to the peaceful program. The state, for example, can become directly involved in prospecting, mining, and processing activities; it is obviously required to launch a vast research and developmental effort. This effort, in turn, may induce the state to embark on undertakings for the commercial applications of nuclear energy. Of course, the peculiarly hazardous nature of the substances and processes used necessitate a continuous regulatory surveillance of every aspect of the program, whether it is private or public.

Can one organization effectively administer these assorted activities? Among the countries included in this survey, Canada and Japan have acknowledged the uniqueness of the several parts of the program by creating separate administrative entities for each activity. The other countries have attempted to keep all the activities under one agency. All countries, at the same time, have sought to ease the administrative load by transferring parts of the program to private concerns. But this decision has, in turn, necessitated making organizational arrangements for fostering collaboration of government, industry, and universities. Moreover, in practice, it has proven impossible to include all elements associated with atomic energy in one self-contained department. Other departments having regulatory or operational responsibilities in such fields as health, labor, trade, and other areas of scientific endeavor inevitably cut across the jurisdictional areas assigned to nuclear-energy establishments. Hence, the organization has also had to meet the urgent need for co-ordination that this poses.

Apart from the problem of co-ordination, the decision to set up special nuclear-energy agencies also imposes the need to consider how they may best be fitted into the over-all structure of executive and legislative controls. Here, as one might expect, the solutions adopted reflect the variations in constitutional and institutional arrangements which are peculiar to each country. Nevertheless, there is a common problem confronting all nations, regardless of detailed variations in the organizational pattern: how adequate are the controls exercised by laymen over policies and programs in this complex, somewhat esoteric field which, by its nature, is dominated by the scientist and technician? Thus, the old problem of expert-to-amateur relationships is accentuated and possibly exacerbated by the mounting importance of science in government and in the life of each nation.

We turn now to a survey of the atomic-energy organizations themselves. Any writer in the field of public administration knows that it is not easy to stir enthusiasm for the detailed scrutiny of organizational charts. Yet, just as it is necessary to apply some imagination in order to visualize the relation of building plans to the functions of buildings, so the student of organization must seek to establish the appropriateness of the organization chart to the purpose for which it presumably was designed; he is also concerned with whether an organization fits congenially into the total governmental structure.

In the case of the organizations for implementing the nuclear-energy program, there were a number of common design specifications that had to be met by all countries. First, the organization had to be flexible. The full peacetime potential of the atom was an unknown quantity, and the administrative structure had to be capable of adapting to changes in program and purposes. Flexibility was also essential if the incredibly rapid growth of functions and staff was to be properly absorbed. Second, the mixture of pure and applied sciences had to be contained in one structure, with the prospect of the same organization's managing substantial industrial undertakings once research had opened up applied commercial opportunities. Third, the program was bound to bring together possibly the largest single assemblage of scientists, engineers, and technicians with which governments had even been forced to contend. Fourth, the state's financial involvement was clearly to be very large and prolonged, with little expectation of substantial short-run returns on the investment. Finally, the organization had to be geared to meet the public's legitimate concern over the little-known hazards of the substances and processes used. The description that follows is intended primarily to show how well the various organizations have met these general specifications.

The United States. In 1946, the critical organizational decision confronting the authorities in the United States was whether the new agency (which was generally considered necessary for managing the nuclear-energy program) should be headed by a single administrator or should be set up as a collegial body.

It is common practice in the United States to place single administrators with extensive operational responsibilities at the
head of agencies, and this view had some support in the planning
stages. However, both the president and his chief advisor on organizational questions, the director of the Bureau of the Budget,
favored a commission. In the event, the 1946 act provided for
a five-man civilian Atomic Energy Commission appointed by the
president for five-year terms. Underlining the intention to accord the commission a status somewhat independent of the chief
executive, the legislation further provided that removal of the
members could be only "for cause."

This form of organization is by no means unique, and there
were special circumstances at the time which argued strongly in
its favor. The scientific community itself was disturbed by the
destructive potential of the bomb. They, together with the general public, were reluctant to entrust the awesome responsibility
for decisions in this novel and disturbing field to a single administrator. It was realized at the time that the choice of a commission "diffused responsibility" and would "slow down the decision
process"; nevertheless, these defects were regarded as a necessary
"sacrifice" in order to avoid concentration of responsibility in one
person.[1] Under the circumstances, it was thought better to entrust this untried field to a commission of equals, each member
of which could bring his experience and judgment to bear on
the issues involved.

Reflecting even more strongly the antipathy to conferring
all power on one authority even when headed by a commission,
the Act of 1946 provided for a Joint Congressional Committee
on Atomic Energy composed of nine members from each chamber. Over the years this committee has exercised its statutory
power over "all bills, resolutions or other matters . . . relating
primarily to the Commission or to the development, use or control of atomic energy" in such a fashion as to make it an extremely
active partner of the commission even in the exercise of purely

[1] These, at least, are the views of the atomic-energy commissioners themselves in a letter dated May 11, 1962, quoted by John W. Finney in *The New
York Times*, "A.E.C. Is Weighing Abolishing Itself," November 18, 1962.

FIG 1. ATOMIC-ENERGY ORGANIZATION
IN THE UNITED STATES

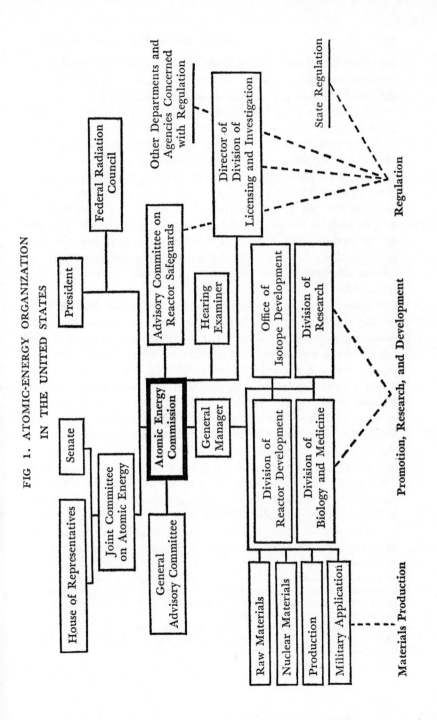

executive functions.[2] This unique departure from the traditional
separation of powers demonstrates in a most dramatic fashion
the unwillingness of Congress to entrust the development of this
new source of energy completely to an agency described by one
representative as the most totalitarian commission in all history.[3]

The strictly military aspects of the commission's activities
are subject to presidential directives, authorized by the Atomic
Energy Act.[4] Although some have held that these provisions
limit the president's authority to the matters specified in the
sections, the prevailing interpretation is that presidential control extends, as it does in other commissions, to the whole range
of the commission's programs. Practice appears to confirm this
interpretation, and, to assist the president in formulating regulations covering radiation hazards, a special advisory Federal
Radiation Council has been created.

The over-all organizational arrangements for dealing with
atomic energy must include the many departments and agencies
whose normal responsibilities may be peripheral to those of the
commission's but do cut across them at certain points. On the
operational side, the chief agency involved is the Defense Department; on the regulatory side, the Maritime Administration, the
Bureau of Mines, the Geological Survey, the National Bureau
of Standards, and the departments of Health, Education, and
Welfare, Labor, and Agriculture all have some connection; on
the scientific and developmental side are involved the Office of
Science and Technology, the Federal Council for Science and
Technology, the National Academy of Sciences, and the National
Science Foundation, all of whom are responsible for advising on
or co-ordinating the total scientific effort of the nation.

The Atomic Energy Commission is designed to reflect the
three main activities of the agency. The main operational func-

---

[2] See the excellent analysis of this committee by Harold P. Green and Alan
Rosenthal, "Fusion of Government Power," *Bulletin of the Atomic Scientists*,
XVIII (June 1962), 12–16, and *idem, Government of the Atom: The Integra-
tion of Powers* (New York: Atherton Press, 1963).

[3] *The Congressional Record*, XCII, as quoted by Hans Kruse, *Legal
Aspects of the Peaceful Utilization of Atomic Energy* (Berlin: Verlag Neue
Wirtschafts-Briefe Herne, 1960), p. 31.

[4] § 41 (b) and § 91 (b) (1).

tions are the procurement of raw materials and the operation of facilities for the production of fissionable materials and atomic weapons; for these functions the divisions of Raw Materials, Production, and Military Application are responsible. Promotional functions include the development of nuclear power and commercial applications of radioisotopes; the Division of Reactor Development and the Office of Isotope Development are concerned with these matters. The third and most rapidly growing area of activity involves regulatory action to protect the public from hazards; this responsibility is shared by the Division of Licensing and Regulation, the Inspection Division and the Office of Health and Safety. Until recently all divisions and offices reported to the commission through the general manager, but a reorganization establishing an Office of the Director of Regulation which reports directly to the commission occurred in 1961.[5]

Do these organizational arrangements meet all the special requirements and problems encountered by the atomic-energy program? An answer can be provided only by noting what appear to be the major trouble spots.

The first trouble spot is the form of organization at the top. There is renewed agitation to adopt a single administrator in order to provide more satisfactory and unified direction for the vast operational and promotional activities, which have grown tremendously since the commission was formed. Even the commissioners appear to support the change, although the matter is still far from settled.[6] A resolution of this issue may well depend on what decision is taken on the present combination of regulatory and operating activities of the commission. The problem is created by an arrangement which seeks to make one agency responsible for all major aspects of the atomic-energy program. An organizational modus vivendi has thus far preserved an un-

---

[5] For a good sketch of the organization and operation of the commission, see Staff of the Joint Committee on Atomic Energy, *Improving the AEC Regulatory Process*, 87th Cong., 1st Sess. (1961), pp. 4–14.

[6] Finney, *op. cit.* Harold P. Green notes that the original act provided for presidential appointment of the general manager as well as the commissioners; in 1950, however, the commissioners were empowered to appoint the general manager, thereby divorcing the president from the operating side of the AEC's activities ("Atomic Energy: Commission or Administrator?" *Bulletin of the Atomic Scientists*, XVIII [December 1962], 33–37).

easy balance by achieving separation of the regulatory and operational-promotional duties within the commission. Should it
be decided to revert to a single administrator, this combination
may prove less acceptable, and a separate regulatory body might
well result.[7]

The need to preserve flexibility is one of the major requirements of any atomic-energy organization. The institution of a
separate agency appears to have provided a satisfactory means of
coping with the rapid growth which has characterized all atomic-
energy programs. The crucial test of flexibility, however, is the
capacity to manage funds and manpower. On the financial side,
the unusual technique of voting so-called no-term money to the
commission seems ideally suited to the operational needs of an
agency whose costly projects often take years to complete. By
this means, the commission has escaped the confines of the budgetary year and is able to plan on a long-term basis. Less success has attended the management of personnel, for the commission has been bound rather closely to civil service procedures and
salaries, which place it at a disadvantage in competing with industry and others for the scarce talents required in a scientific
enterprise of such dimensions.[8] It is probable that difficulties in
recruiting or retaining qualified scientists and engineers for
government service have induced the Atomic Energy Commission
to make extensive use of the contract for research and development and for undertaking certain operating responsibilities. But

[7] For an opposing view, see the comments dated April 12, 1961, to the Joint
Congressional Committee on Atomic Energy, *Improving the AEC . . .*,
op. cit.: "The discussion group generally held that the regulatory problem
is unrelated to whether the AEC is headed by a single administrator rather
than a commission" (p. 14). Other views generally favored an internal reorganization of the commission to effect a clear separation of the regulatory
function.

[8] A number of reports on this subject reveal the concern in the United
States to secure a proper supply of qualified scientific and technical man
power not only for the atomic-energy program, but for the growing scientific
requirements of the nation. See, for example, *Report of the Defense Advisory
Committee on Professional and Technical Compensation*, (Washington, D.C.:
Government Printing Office, 1957), Vol. II; The President's Committee on
Scientists and Engineers, *Final Report to the President*, (1958); and an un-
dated mimeographed report of the National Advisory Committee on Aeronautics, *Crisis in the Recruitment and Retention of Scientists and Engineers
in the Federal Government*.

the reliance on contractual labor generates fresh problems, for, if most qualified experts are outside the government, it is difficult to see how an agency like the Atomic Energy Commission can establish the proper priorities or appraise the quality of the results. By the same token, extensive use of consultants enhances the prospect of conflict-of-interest situations, in which the same people may be concerned with the direction of governmental contract projects while advising the government on the allocation of these contracts.[9]

In short, although the organization originally devised to carry out the atomic-energy program has been generally effective for marshaling the resources required to establish a new technology, the present combination of wholly unrelated functions in one agency produces problems that indicate adjustments will have to be made.

The United Kingdom. Responsibility for all research and development aspects of the atomic-energy program in Britain is concentrated in a single organization, the United Kingdom Atomic Energy Authority. Despite the popularity of the public corporation—a form the Labour government deemed most appropriate for the newly nationalized industries—the atomic-energy program was initially contained in the normal departmental structure. However, in 1954, the rapidly increasing burdens of the program were shifted from the Ministry of Supply to a special corporate agency. The committee which was set up to consider "the future organization of the atomic energy project" explained that the change was necessary because, "As the industrial uses of atomic energy become relatively more prominent, the case for a form of control . . . which is more akin to the structure of a big industrial organization than to that of a government Department becomes increasingly strong." [10]

This conclusion was formally confirmed in the Atomic Energy Authority Act of 1954, and the new authority assumed charge of operations in July, 1954. The original governing

[9] These points are forcibly made by Jerome B. Weisner, director of the Office of Science and Technology, in a speech, extracts from which appeared in *Bulletin of the Atomic Scientists,* XVIII (November 1962), 42–46.

[10] United Kingdom House of Commons, *op. cit.,* paragraph 11.

board comprised the three heads of existing establishments: Sir John Cockcroft in basic research at Harwell, Sir William Penney on military developments at Aldermaston, and Sir Christopher Hinton on industrial production at Risley in Lancashire. These men, with Sir Edwin (now Lord) Plowden, the former chief economic planner of the Labour government, as the first chairman and Sir Donald Perrott, a career civil servant in charge of finance and administration, made up the permanent members. There were also three part-time members. A 1959 amendment to the legislation provided for a larger board of up to fifteen members; currently the board operates with twelve, equally divided between permanent and part-time members. The former constitute a management committee, known as the Atomic Energy Executive, which meets at more frequent intervals than the full board.

Since 1959, the ministry responsible for the authority has been the Ministry for Science (a position held by the lord president of the council). Prior to 1959, atomic energy came under the minister of supply (1945–1953), the lord president (1954–1956), and the prime minister himself (1957–1959). The minister for science's authority embraces the appointment of board members, their terms of service, their salaries (in consultation with the Treasury), and the power to give the authority such directions as he may think fit.[11] The last power has been employed infrequently, although on more occasions than has been generally true of the nationalized industries.

In the rather small office of the Ministry for Science, the Atomic Energy Division makes up about half the staff. It has been deliberate policy not to set up an elaborate Whitehall bureaucracy that would duplicate or attempt to check the work of the authority itself. There are no scientists in the division, and the authority can, if it sees fit, deal directly with the minister or the heads of nationalized boards. The chairman of the authority attends meetings of the Cabinet Committee on Atomic Energy and has free access to the minister for science and even the prime minister. He and his colleagues attend other minis-

---

[11] The Atomic Energy Authority Act, c. 32, 2–3 Eliz. II (1954), § 3 (2–3).

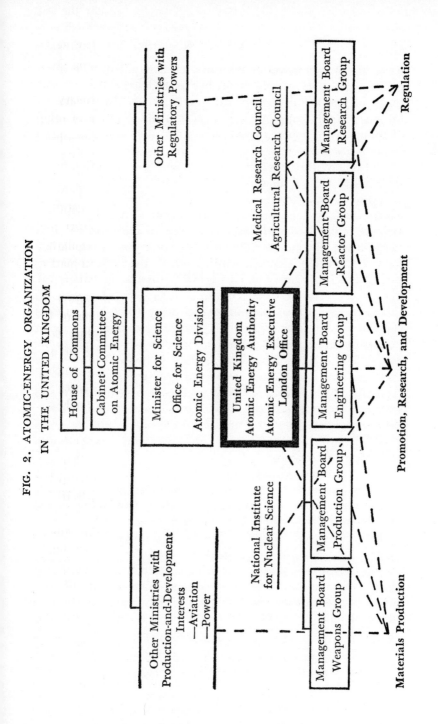

FIG. 2. ATOMIC-ENERGY ORGANIZATION
IN THE UNITED KINGDOM

House of Commons

Cabinet Committee
on Atomic Energy

Other Ministries with
Regulatory Powers

Minister for Science
Office for Science
Atomic Energy Division

Other Ministries with
Production-and-Development
Interests
—Aviation
—Power

United Kingdom
Atomic Energy Authority
Atomic Energy Executive
London Office

National Institute
for Nuclear Science

Medical Research Council
Agricultural Research Council

Management Board
Weapons Group

Management Board
Production Group

Management Board
Engineering Group

Management Board
Reactor Group

Management Board
Research Group

Materials Production

Promotion, Research, and Development

Regulation

terial or official committee meetings when required. The infor-
mality of all these arrangements has been described by the secretary of the Atomic Energy Division in the minister's office as
follows: "We do not go through a solemn and stately passing up
of things to the top of the Authority and then a passing down
through my office." [12]

Although this top-level organization has the primary responsibility for the atomic-energy program, a number of other
departments and agencies are concerned with one or more aspects
which come within their respective orbits. The Ministry for
Defence is involved with military aspects of the program, as is
the Ministry of Aviation. The Ministry for Power is responsible
for the Electricity Council, which controls the entire nationalized electricity industry and its growing interest in power produced by nuclear reactors. Over the whole field of regulation,
there is a similar dispersion of responsibility which is in marked
contrast to the situation in the United States. The minister of
power, for example, is concerned with the safety of power reactors. The regulation of other hazards is in the hands of the
ministers for agriculture, town and country planning, Scotland; the Medical and Agricultural Research councils are also
involved. Several advisory committees, notably the Nuclear
Safety Advisory Committee and the Radioactive Substances Advisory Committee, are associated with these ministries for health
and safety regulations.

The internal organization of the Atomic Energy Authority
differs markedly from that in other countries, but is obviously
closely modeled on the arrangements which have been worked
out for such nationalized industries as coal, gas, and electricity,
each of which has a central office and a number of area or regional management boards. In the case of the Atomic Energy
Authority, the organizational division is based on function rather
than area: there are now five groups—research, reactors, engineering, production, and weapons. Each group has its own
board of managers appointed by the main board and enjoying
substantial day-to-day autonomy. Representatives from the main

---

[12] Select Committee on Estimates of the House of Commons, *5th Report
and Minutes of Evidence,* Evid., Q. 9 (Sess. 1958–1959).

board and from the groups sit on each of the group management boards. The main board is serviced by a small London office which performs certain common services—notably the procurement of uranium—and handles the financial and Parliamentary business of the authority.

This functional subdivision with semi-autonomous management boards responsible for each function goes well beyond any of the other countries' organizational arrangements for administering the many activities of a total atomic-energy program through one agency. That these arrangements are not entirely satisfactory is revealed by the extensive number of co-ordinating committees at all levels.

As was previously observed, flexibility to meet the problems of rapid growth, staffing, and finance is a prime requisite for such an organization. It is customary to provide this flexibility by granting semi-autonomous status to the agency involved. In the case of the Atomic Energy Authority, however, at least three important special features necessitated certain modifications in the usual form of nationalized industries. The authority would be concerned with the deadliest of all weapons; its peaceful functions would be charged with most tremendous political and international implications; and, for as long as could be foreseen, it would almost entirely depend on public funds. This combination of factors necessitated a somewhat tighter system of financial and executive control than usual for nationalized industries.

In broad terms, the legal corporate status conferred on the authority has the same consequences that it has for any other similar administrative entity; it possesses all the powers and obligations attaching to such bodies in English law, and, in particular, it can claim none of the Crown's privileges in legal proceedings (as would an ordinary department). As in a regular department, however, the provisions of the Official Secrets Acts apply to all members of the board, its employees, and all land and premises under the authority's control.

Although the authority controls its own staff of some 40,000 employees, many of them formerly held civil service positions, and this has tended to govern personnel policies. Salaries and wages form an item in the authority's estimates of expenditure,

which, like those for any department, have to be submitted to
the Treasury for approval. The salary rates for senior officials
tend to be higher than those in the civil service, but the authority has been enjoined by the government not to pay salaries
that are seriously out of line with those paid by other public
corporations. At the lower level, too, salaries must not widely
diverge from those in the civil service. These restrictions, as in
the United States, have hampered the authority's ability to compete with industry for scientific and technical personnel. It is
probable, however, that staffing difficulties are mainly attributable to the national shortage of qualified personnel in these
fields. Wastage rates in the authority are not published, but the
Select Committee on Estimates was privately shown the figures
and was apparently satisfied that they were not unduly high. In
any event, the close working partnership which the authority
seeks to maintain with industry implies a good deal of cross-
fertilization through exchange and transfer of staff between the
public and private sectors. Good labor relations have been preserved with the industrial employees, who make up more than
half of the authority's staff, because union bargaining procedures
comparable with those in private industry are available.

Possibly the most serious challenge to management stems
from the rapid expansion of staff—a doubling in size over a
recent five-year period. Early in 1959, the authority adopted a
policy for containing this expansion: for the next three years
the annual rate of growth on the civil research and developmental side was to be restricted to eight per cent.

The authority has been granted even less freedom to ma-
neuver in the area of finance. It relies almost exclusively on
Parliamentary appropriations, which are voted to the minister
for science and then re-allocated to the authority. The revenues
that it earns are paid into the Exchequer by virtue of a ministerial directive of 1954. Treasury control is much stricter than
it is for the nationalized industries because the authority is
financed for operating, as well as for capital, expenditures by
the Exchequer. Although this financial control is designed to
give the Treasury a strong voice in determining general policy,
the pressure to go "all out" on the atomic-energy program has

always ensured sufficient funds for the authority. A more significant limitation on the pace of the authority's program has been the scarcity of skilled manpower and physical resources.

In summary, the decision to establish a special agency to assume full responsibility for atomic energy in the United Kingdom has resulted in the creation of a public corporation with less managerial freedom, in form at least, than has been accorded other nationalized industries. More detailed investigation reveals that the authority is by no means the sole command in many matters, particularly in the regulatory side of the program. This dispersion of responsibility produces problems of co-ordination, and the mechanisms for meeting these problems proliferate at all levels. The adequacy of the machinery for balancing the claims of the atomic-energy program against those of other important scientific undertakings has also been the subject of recent critical comment.

Internally, the organization of the authority appears to be a model of coherence and logic when compared with other countries. But in an agency that has had to absorb a phenomenally rapid growth, there are bound to be difficulties. Recently, for example, *The Economist,* calling the authority an "awful warning," asked: "What are all these people doing? Should someone find out and tell them to stop?" [13] In broad terms, the answer is that, since the authority's objectives are set by the government, "these people" are doing what they are told and, if anyone is to tell them to stop, it must be the government. By now, however, the structure appears to have become sufficiently stable to warrant a critical evaluation of the whole organization.

France. France has followed the United States and the United Kingdom in seeking to organize the government's portion of the atomic-energy program under one agency. This agency is, in fact, a somewhat unique public body having some of the attributes of the public corporation in Britain and some of the commission in the United States. The special circumstances surrounding the inauguration of the atomic-energy program induced the authorities, as in other countries, to discard the idea

---

[13] *The Economist,* March 25, 1961, p. 1217.

of making the organization an appendage to a regular ministry or another commission without a distinct legal personality. An organization that would be sufficiently stable to survive the vicissitudes of postwar French politics was required. Autonomy was required to obtain such stability, but, at the same time, the agency could not be permitted to operate in complete independence from the executive. The balancing of these two objectives constitutes, of course, the classic paradox of the public corporation: how to combine managerial autonomy and continuity of administration with the political surveillance necessary to preserve responsible administration.

The ordinance of 1945 created an establishment endowed with its own legal personality and with financial and administrative autonomy, but subject to the ultimate control of responsible political authorities. To this end, the founding ordinance placed the Atomic Energy Authority not merely under the control, but also under the direction (*sous l'autorité*) of the president of the provisional government (subsequently the prime minister). A decree of 1951 further declared that "the Authority shall be administered . . . in accordance with general directions of the Government."

The managing board (le Comité de l'Énergie Atomique) of the authority is formally chaired by the prime minister, a minister designated by him, or (since a decree of January, 1951) by the general manager (*l'administrateur général*) of the authority. In practice, the general manager normally presides, and such directions as are required are issued by the minister delegated by the prime minister to act virtually as the minister for atomic energy. The latter also receives annual and special reports from the authority and generally maintains a continuing interest in its affairs. A Ministerial Committee on Atomic Energy, presided over by the prime minister and representing the ministerial heads of departments having an interest in atomic-energy matters, acts as a sort of appellate tribunal whenever the managerial board of the authority is divided on policy questions.

Perhaps the most novel feature of the authority is the managerial dyarchy located at the top of the structure. One of the most vexing and controversial issues emerging from the mas-

FIG. 3. ATOMIC-ENERGY ORGANIZATION IN FRANCE

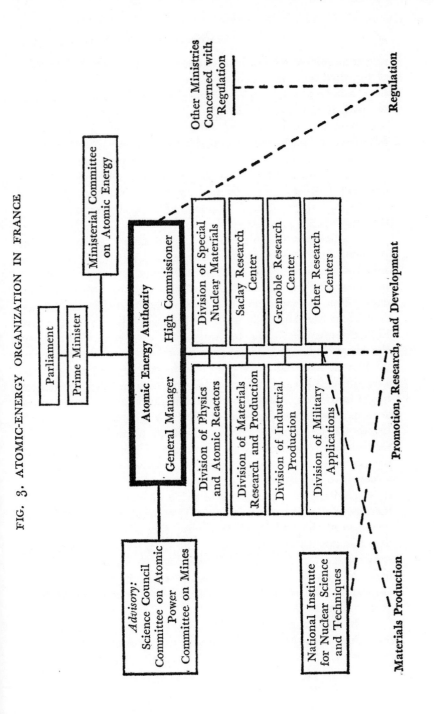

sive intrusion of science into government has been the question of top direction: should it be placed in the hands of a scientist or of a lay administrator? In France, the problem has been side-stepped, if not resolved, by placing both types of officer in the top command. On one hand, administrative and financial tasks have been vested in the general manager; on the other hand, the scientist occupying the post of high commissioner (*haut commissaire*) has been freed from tasks which are foreign to his training and temperament and has been left in charge of only the strictly scientific and developmental activities of the authority.

Unquestionably, this solution was dictated as much by the personal attributes of the first incumbents as by any considerations of organizational logic. Raoul Dautry, the first general manager, was known to be a sound administrator who could be counted on to supplement and possibly contain the scientifically competent but politically unstable Frédéric Joliot-Curie, the first high commissioner. The teaming up of two equals to manage the sprawling and rapidly growing program of the authority might well have had paralyzing consequences. The general manager through his power to appoint and his control over finances might have brought matters to a standstill by refusing to sanction an appointment or payment of the high commissioner. According to the founding ordinance, the high commissioner was, in fact, given pre-eminence, but the decree of 1951 transferred this pre-eminence to the general manager. In practice, the importance attached to the scientific and developmental side of the authority's activities has tended to give pride of place in major policy matters to the high commissioner. The equable and friendly association of the individuals who have successively held these offices has made the system work. The fact, too, that over a sixteen-year period there have been very few changes in the incumbents has given a notable continuity to their direction of the authority's affairs; in all, only five men have been involved, four of whom enjoyed long tenures.

The two managerial heads and the chairman (who may be the prime minister or his ministerial delegate) are the most important members of the authority's governing board. At the outset, four other members, representing science, industry, and government made up the full board. The number and composition of the board members have been altered several times, but now, in addition to its three chief members, the board consists of eight members appointed for five-year terms. The board meets not less than once a month and can be convened at any time on the request of the managerial heads of the authority. Decisions are taken by majority vote, the chairman having the right to cast the deciding vote. In instances when the general manager happens, as is normally the case, to be the presiding officer, matters on which the vote has been evenly divided must be re-examined under the chairmanship of the prime minister or the ministerial delegate. When a majority of the board is opposed to the views of either the high commissioner or the general manager, the dispute is arbitrated by the ministerial committee, with a final determination by the prime minister.

The responsibilities of the board are comprehensive. It defines the policies of the authority in research, manufacturing, and other works; it controls the two executive officers of the authority by considering and approving their annual accounts, forecasts of revenue and expenditure, certain purchases and sales of real property; it considers any matter submitted by the prime minister or by the two executive officers. It is clear that the two unusually powerful executive officers tend to dominate the board in setting the policy of the authority and in directing its operations. In one sense they are agents of the governing board, but it is apparent that they are more than agents when both sit on the board and one customarily presides over it. In case of disagreement with the other board members, they both have access to the Ministerial Committee on Atomic Energy and the prime minister.

As in other countries, the top structure for directing the atomic-energy program is supplemented by various other administrative entities. Research and training in the universities, for example, are co-ordinated by a separate, though closely related, body, the National Institute for Nuclear Science and Techniques. The authority, with other high government and university officials, is represented on its governing body. The Science

Council, broadly representing the entire scientific community in France, has a general responsibility for co-ordinating the nation's scientific efforts. The Committee for Mines and the Committee for Industrial Equipment—the latter with an important adjunct, the Consultative Commission for the Production of Nuclear Power—have advisory relationships with the authority and in some areas promulgate and supervise the enforcement of the necessary regulations. There is also a Consultative Commission on Marketing on which the authority is represented. It hardly needs to be added that the War Department is closely concerned with all military applications under study and development by the authority and that in regulatory matters affecting health, labor conditions, and the like the regular ministries play an important part.

The internal organization of the authority's servicing and operating units reveals a pattern similar to that adopted by regular ministries, but with an obvious intent to separate scientific and technical operations in the various branches (*directions*) from the purely administrative and common service functions, under the respective supervision of the high commissioner and the general manager. None of these subdivisions possesses a separate legal personality, for all are subordinate to the central administration of the authority. The numerous scientific and technical establishments have their own directors who have some managerial freedom, but, among the directors, the authority has encountered dissatisfaction with the co-ordinating controls exercised at authority headquarters.[14]

In personnel and financial matters, the semi-autonomous status granted the authority has, as in other countries, enabled it to build an impressive establishment and pioneer an imposing scientific and industrial effort in a few years. The staff has increased from 236 in 1946 to over 14,000 in 1960. To these should be added another 2,000 university probationers and temporary employees in the mining enterprises outside metropolitan France. These personnel, with the exception of the two executive heads, are covered by the laws relating to industrial and commercial

---

. .[14] See Bertrand Goldschmidt, "The French Atomic Energy Program," *Bulletin of the Atomic Scientists*, XVIII (October 1962), 46–48.

undertakings and are not part of the civil service proper.[15] Salaries at the top are equal to those paid in the nationalized electricity industry or, in the case of mining, accord with the regulations of the mining statute. Although the authority is not obliged to enter into collective agreements with its employees, since 1950 their virtual equivalents have been concluded with the employees. Special provisions have been incorporated into these agreements to ensure secrecy and security in the sensitive areas of operations. Every employee is required to sign an agreement to preserve professional secrecy in the activities of the authority which are not publicized, and this obligation continues in force after the employee leaves the authority. Normal recruitment examinations used by the civil service are not employed by the authority, which uses special security screening procedures. Thus, the authority has complete discretion in hiring or rejecting applicants.

As in the United Kingdom the fiscal autonomy of the authority has had to be hedged a great deal because of the almost total reliance on public funds for all parts of the program. The authority receives funds from three sources—regular appropriations to cover operating and capital expenditures, loans from the Economic and Social Development Fund, and small revenues from commercial sales of its own products. The total budget has grown from a modest 5,000,000 N.F. in 1946 to 1,240,000,000 in 1961. Over 84 per cent of the total in 1961 came from appropriations charged to the budget of the prime minister; nearly 10 per cent from the Development Fund; and the remainder from the authority's own resources. If one adds the money expended on the military aspects of the nuclear-energy program in 1961, approximately 5 per cent of the budget is devoted to the entire program.[16] Even this figure is incomplete, for an additional 200,000,000 N.F. is being annually spent by the French Electricity Authority for nuclear power stations.

As these sums have mounted, increasing attention has been given to systematizing budgetary procedures and applying appro-

---

[15] On the complexities of the law covering staff of this type, consult Brian Chapman, *The Profession of Government* (London: Allen and Unwin, 1959), pp. 54–56.

[16] See *Débats parlementaires, 1961*, November 12, 1960.

priate controls. To this end, two five-year plans have already been implemented, and a third, to carry forward to 1965, has been recently adopted. Annual budgets, laid down in accordance with these plans, are submitted by the board of the authority for the approval of the prime minister and the minister of finance. The existence of the plans is particularly useful for an agency whose programs often take several years to complete and who would otherwise have to plan on a hand-to-mouth basis.

Although the authority has been specifically excluded from the various financial ordinances governing other autonomous state enterprises and state-assisted undertakings, since 1947 detailed statements on personnel expenditures and real property transactions have been subjected to the same scrutiny as those of other public undertakings. A financial control mission examines the accounts and annual balance sheets on behalf of the Ministry of Finance. These are audited by the commission for auditing the accounts of public enterprises, a body attached to the general Audit Office. Its reports are presented to the legislature, where atomic-energy matters come before the Assembly's Commission on Economic and Cultural Affairs and the Senate's Commission on Production and Exchanges.

Canada. Canada and Japan are alike in having allocated atomic-energy activities to more than one organization. There are three specialized bodies wholly concerned with nuclear energy in Canada. Eldorado Mining and Refining Ltd. is essentially responsible for procurement of uranium and is responsible for all processes from preliminary exploration, through mining, processing, and refining of ores, to manufacture of the metal. Atomic Energy of Canada Ltd. handles research and development. The Atomic Energy Control Board is primarily concerned with regulation.

The resort to non-departmental forms of organization has created in Canada, as it has elsewhere, an untidy situation in which the lines of authority and responsibility to Parliament and the executive are complex and somewhat devious. In the case of the three agencies concerned with atomic energy, there is more than the usual loose fit into the conventional pattern of minis-

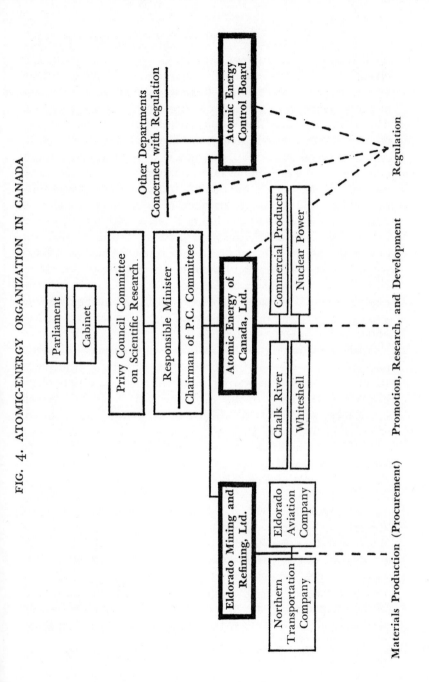

FIG. 4. ATOMIC-ENERGY ORGANIZATION IN CANADA

terial responsibility. In 1954, an amendment to the Atomic Energy Control Act sought to clarify the situation by having all three agencies report to the minister holding the position of chairman of the Committee of the Privy Council on Scientific Research. This minister is also responsible, in that capacity, for the government's chief research agency, the National Research Council.

These arrangements are designed to preserve at least a token allegiance to the doctrine of ministerial responsibility, but there are two reasons for questioning the effectiveness of the co-ordination and control that they can achieve. In recent years the committee has not met at all and has met only at rare intervals since its inception. Second, the minister presently acting as chairman carries the portfolio of an active department (Veterans Affairs) whose operations have nothing to do with science in general or with atomic energy in particular. In practice, the three agencies enjoy substantial latitude to develop policy, restrained only by the necessity of securing cabinet approval for major activities and of obtaining the necessary funds.

The organization for the two operating agencies—Eldorado and Atomic Energy of Canada—follows a pattern which was widely used during the war for conducting a great variety of industrial undertakings of the government. The so-called Crown companies—some thirty of which were created mainly at the instigation of the late C. D. Howe, a prominent industrialist and a powerful member of the cabinet—were chosen to administer the atomic-energy program.

Eldorado Mining and Refining Ltd., the first of these, was incorporated in 1945 under the Dominion Companies Act of 1934. In accordance with the terms of that act, the directors of the company were issued qualifying shares, and the rest of the share capital was registered in the name of the responsible minister in trust of Her Majesty the Queen in right of Canada. The company operates under authority of patent issued by the secretary of state, an order in council setting out the responsibilities of the company, and an agreement between the minister and the directors.[17] It is understood that the directors' qualifying shares

---

[17] Authorized share capital was set at 110,000 shares of no par value; 70,500 shares have been issued, only seven of which are held by the present di-

are endorsed over to the minister—an unequivocal indication of where final control resides. Nevertheless, according to the Financial Administration Act of 1951, the company is scheduled as a "proprietary corporation," the most independent form, entitled to its own assets and empowered to formulate its own operating budget without appropriations from Parliament.[18] With the exception of the annual cabinet approval required for capital budgets, the company generally enjoys freedom to manage its own financial affairs. This financial freedom has been more meaningful for Eldorado than for most other incorporated governmental enterprises because over the years it has readily met expenses out of revenues and has not had to fall back on Parliament for financial support. This extremely healthy financial position is reflected in cumulative dividends amounting to some $20,000,000 paid to the government, another $17,000,000 paid in income taxes, and a deposit for working capital of over $13,000,000 (December, 1960).[19]

The mining and exploration activities of the company have been concentrated in the remote northern regions of Canada, where the original expropriated properties were located. Two wholly owned subsidiary transportation companies—Eldorado Aviation Ltd. (1953) and Northern Transportation Company Ltd. (for water transport)—have been annexed to Eldorado in order to facilitate these northern operations. Total staff, at seasonal peak, numbers over 1,600 persons.

The other major activity of Eldorado derives from its being the monopoly producer of the refined uranium. All ore, whether privately produced or extracted from the company's own mines, is sent to the company's Port Hope refinery. In 1953, the company

rectors to qualify them under the Companies Act. Total government investment amounts to over $9,000,000, of which more than $5,000,000 was required to reimburse the private shareholders after expropriation in 1944. In 1949, $1,000,000 of capital stock was redeemed.
[18] Details on the Financial Administration Act and Crown companies are to be found in J. E. Hodgetts, "The Public Corporation in Canada," in W. Friedmann (ed.), *The Public Corporation. A Comparative Symposium* ("University of Toronto Law School Comparative Law Series," Vol. I [Toronto: The Carswell Company Limited, 1954]), pp. 51–92.
[19] See House of Commons, Canada, Special Committee on Research, *Minutes of Proceedings and Evidence* (Ottawa: Queen's Printer, 1961), pp. 16–19, 22.

created a special research and development division which embraces a wide range of ore-dressing and metal-fabrication processes. A sales promotion division is joined to these activities of the company.

Atomic Energy of Canada Ltd., the second of the specialized operating agencies, is also a Crown company. Although the original Atomic Energy Act of 1946 visualized the creation of companies to exploit the peacetime uses of the atom, it was not until 1952 that research and development work on atomic energy— hitherto conducted as part of the activities of the National Research Council—was segregated for special attention. The company that took over these responsibilities was, like Eldorado Mining and Refining, incorporated under the Companies Act, each of the eleven members of its board being given a qualifying share. The directors are appointed by the government to be broadly representative of the utilities, banking, engineering, and academic professions. The full board meets quarterly, but an executive committee meets more frequently.

Like Eldorado, the company confronts an imposing problem of supervising from its Ottawa headquarters the activities of units physically scattered and well removed from the center. Research is located at Chalk River, 150 miles upriver from the capital and, more recently, half a continent away at Whiteshell in Manitoba. Development work on nuclear-generated power has necessitated locating the Nuclear Power Division in Toronto close to the provincially run utility with which the company is cooperating on the first major installation.

The financing of Atomic Energy of Canada has produced more complications than has that of Eldorado, largely because its operations are far from self-supporting. Less than ten per cent of total financial requirements are obtained from the company's own commercial sales; for the remainder, it must rely on Parliamentary appropriations, annually submitted and approved much as for an ordinary department. Expenditures on research are provided out of ordinary vote and written off each year, whereas expenditures which have commercial potentialities are capitalized. On the research side, expenditures are divided into requirements for operations and research capital. In addition, requirements for fundable and working capital are prepared; after deducting estimated revenues from operations, the net requirements are submitted to Parliament for approval.

Control of the budget is maintained by submitting the estimates to the responsible minister, who, in turn, seeks Treasury Board approval of them. Individual capital projects costing over $5,000 require approval of the Board of Directors; the total capital program must be submitted to Treasury Board through the minister. Expenditures on capital works are covered by issuing capital stock or other obligations of the company. As of 1960, some 54,000 shares had been issued out of an authorized total of 75,000 common shares of no par value. In effect then, Parliament provides the company with most of the money needed for its program and takes back securities for the things that may be sold, as distinct from the research and development work, from which no revenues result.[20]

Within the company, the distinction between revenue-producing and non-productive operations is preserved by financing the Commercial Products Division strictly along commercial lines. It receives advances from the main office and pays for products and services provided by the company out of revenues from the sale of its products. The price charged does not accurately reflect all real costs, but, on the basis of current accounting procedures, this division shows a modest profit on its commercial operations.[21]

These varied provisions for financing the company reflect the fact that it is involved in two distinct operations. On the one hand, it is administering a large, specialized research and development program from which little or no direct financial return can be expected. On the other, it is conducting industrial

---

[20] A clear outline of the financial arrangements and of the total expenditures for each category of research and capital costs is found in Canada, House of Commons, Special Committee on Research, *Minutes of Proceedings and Evidence* (Ottawa: Queen's Printer, 1960), pp. 180, 292–297.

[21] The sales force of the Commercial Products Division has had to find external markets to absorb the bulk of its products since the Canadian market accounts for less than 10 per cent of the total. About half the sales are to the United States, the remainder go to over fifty other countries. In 1959–1960, a profit of some $400,000 was made on a turnover of $3,250,000 (*ibid.*, pp. 270–271).

and commercial operations for which the Crown company form of administration seems ideally suited. However, since the research and developmental activities predominate, the financial independence usually accorded the corporate form of governmental administration has been substantially sacrificed in favor of normal executive and legislative controls. Although accounts are maintained on industrial lines with monthly financial statements, they are scrutinized by the auditor general (parliament's own officer) rather than by an outside commercial firm.

The autonomy enjoyed in managing personnel has enabled the company to adopt a more flexible approach to a mixed scientific and industrial staff than would be permitted by ordinary civil service rules. Since its separation from the National Research Council (which is also autonomous in personnel matters), a close correspondence has been maintained between the salaries of scientific staff employed by the two agencies. Hourly rated employees, who make up 1,200 of the total staff of 2,700, and the technicians and draftsmen are unionized, and their conditions of service are governed by agreements reached through collective bargaining (a departure from normal civil service procedures). Turnover among professional staff is high, but the company regards this as normal and desirable because of its efforts to encourage the training and interchange of staff among its own establishments, the universities, and private industry.

The third agency concerned solely with atomic energy is the Atomic Energy Control Board. It was the first specialized agency to be set up under the 1946 act. It is a five-man board, designated a body corporate, an agent of Her Majesty, able to contract and hold property in the name of Her Majesty.[22] According to the Atomic Energy Control Act of 1946, the board was expected to assume complete control over all matters having to do with atomic energy, but its primary function has been confined to regulation

---

[22] The Atomic Energy Control Act as amended by c. 47, 1953–1954, § 3 (3), reads: "Actions, suits or other legal proceedings in respect of any right or obligation acquired or incurred by the Board on behalf of Her Majesty, whether in its name or in the name of Her Majesty, may be brought or taken by or against the Board in the name of the Board in any court that would have jurisdiction if the Board were not an agent of Her Majesty" (R.S.C. [1952], c. 11).

and control. Three of the five members of the board are drawn from the heads of Eldorado, Atomic Energy of Canada, and the National Research Council. A full-time president and one outside person representing the academic-scientific community complete the board. Its total staff is only eight full-time employees. Clearly, the board is little more than a glorified committee for bringing together those vested with primary operating responsibilities to collaborate in formulating and supervising the regulation of the atomic-energy program.

One obvious consequence of this arrangement is that, in Canada as elsewhere, there is the same reliance on other departments and agencies to help carry out the regulatory aspects of the program. The existence of the board, however, serves to integrate those activities of such departments as Health and Welfare, Trade and Commerce, Mines and Technical Surveys wherever they touch on the regulation of nuclear energy. The most significant organizational gap seems to be at the top of the structure, where ministerial guidance and collective cabinet consideration of the nation's total scientific program are far from adequate.

Japan. The elements making up the atomic-energy program in Japan are allocated to several specialized organs with one body, the Atomic Energy Commission, occupying the central position. Procurement and processing of raw materials are the primary concern of the Atomic Fuel Corporation. Research and development are mainly in the hands of the Japan Atomic Energy Research Institute, with some research also conducted by the Fuel Corporation and the National Institute of Radiological Sciences. Commercial exploitation of nuclear power is vested in the Japan Atomic Power Development Company; procurement and distribution of radioactive isotopes are handled by the Japan Radioisotope Association.

The machinery for integrating and supervising the activities of these agencies consists of the Atomic Energy Bureau, which is perhaps the most important subdivision of the nation's major scientific body, the Japan Science and Technics Agency. Among the agencies responsible for the various parts of the program under the Atomic Energy Commission, the Atomic Energy Bureau is by far the most effective executive instrument.

The commission has functions comparable to those vested in the Canadian Atomic Energy Control Board in that it advises on all nuclear-energy matters and supervises the regulatory side of the program. Unlike its Canadian counterpart, it is placed in direct relationship with the prime minister, to whom its advice is proffered for acceptance or rejection. The other interesting parallel with Canada is that, when the commission was created in Japan, the same query arose as to whether it should be an administrative as well as a policy board. In Canada, as noted, the Control Board never used its statutory power to expand into an administrative organization, but preferred to remain a small policy and regulatory body. The statute creating Japan's Atomic Energy Commission pursued somewhat the same course by restricting its functions to that of advisor on policy with no administrative duties. Unlike Canada, however, the commission was provided with an executive and secretarial arm, the Atomic Energy Bureau. Thus, a direct channel from the policy-maker and the chief executive organ was established and was further confirmed by making the director general of the Science and Technics Agency chairman of the Atomic Energy Commission.

There were special circumstances which dictated the adoption of a small commission consisting of a chairman and six members. Generally, the postwar experience with administrative commissions had led to a decline in their popularity—indeed, most of these commissions, with a few important exceptions like the Fair Trade Commission and the Labour Commission, had ceased to exist by 1955. Their failure could be attributed to lack of strong support from organized interests and the public. In the case of atomic energy, however, there was vociferous public support for an administrative form that would be more responsive to public opinion than the traditional bureaucracy had shown itself to be. Accordingly, the organic legislation declared that the exercise of democratic control over administration for research, development and use of atomic energy was essential. The commission was the form adopted as most likely to reflect and channel the views of the general public and of organized interests.

FIG. 5. ATOMIC-ENERGY ORGANIZATION IN JAPAN

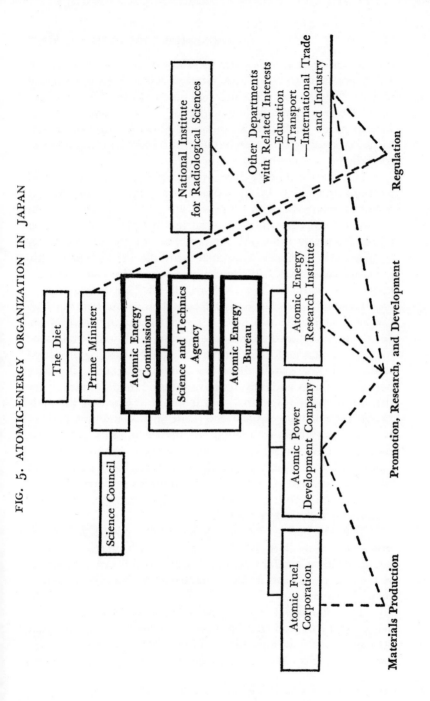

Consequently, in selecting the members of the commission, not only were their technical qualifications taken into account but also their ability to reflect the views of industry, labor, and science. The representative capacities of the commission are restricted by its small size, a limitation which has been overcome to some extent by the appointment of numerous committees of specialists to advise the commission.

The Atomic Energy Bureau is placed in the Science and Technics Agency. It has two functions: it provides the Atomic Energy Commission with an expert secretariat and serves as the central co-ordinator of the specialized agencies and the other ministries whose functions overlap those of the atomic-energy agencies. All estimates concerned with the atomic-energy program are consolidated in the estimates of the bureau and, once they receive legislative approval, are allocated by that agency.

The Japan Atomic Energy Research Institute and the Fuel Corporation are the two most important operating agencies under the general jurisdiction of the bureau. Both were established by separate acts and differ in their mode of financing and legal status. The Research Institute is a mixed undertaking in which both government and industry have invested funds. However, the share of industry is nominal, and it would appear that the main reason for involving private enterprise in this way was to separate the agency from the regular civil service in order to facilitate recruitment of specialists at higher salaries and to secure cooperation with industry. The desire for flexibility in handling personnel—a common theme in the countries surveyed—has not overcome the universal problem of a national shortage of scientific and technical personnel.

The Atomic Fuel Corporation is wholly owned by the government, and the form adopted is in line with practices in other countries like Canada, where an essentially industrial enterprise is deemed to require a departure from the traditional departmental structure.

The commercial exploitation of the power-generating capacity of nuclear reactors has been placed in the hands of the Japan Atomic Power Development Company. This agency is a hybrid bred from the compromise between the private power companies and the Power Resources Development Company which is a mixed private and governmental undertaking. The Atomic Power Development Company is also a mixed enterprise, the governmental portion being fairly small: twenty per cent of the capital in the company is provided by the Power Resources Company which is now almost wholly owned by the government.

The organizational picture is completed by the national Institute of Radiological Sciences, which is one of the national laboratories attached to the Science and Technics Agency. The latter is also involved in controlling the hazards of radioactive materials, for which function it relies on an advisory Radiation Council.

In addition, as in other countries, account must be taken of the several regular departments—the departments of International Trade and Industry, Education, and of Transport—whose work impinges on that of the atomic-energy agencies. In these circumstances and with the numerous specialized participating authorities, a large burden is placed on the co-ordinating mechanisms. In the Atomic Energy Bureau Japan appears to have designed a successful apparatus for bringing all the strands of the program together. And, in the last resort, the legislation underlines the prime minister's special responsibility for making the final determination on all policies concerned with the program, especially with its regulatory features.

Italy. The organization for administering the atomic-energy program in Italy is the least developed and the least specialized of any of the countries previously examined. The delay in establishing a special nuclear-energy agency has enabled the traditional departments to absorb much of the program, so it is likely that the nuclear-energy organization will not attain the powers or extended programs which have been conferred on similar agencies in other countries. Moreover, the dominant position of a few large private industrial concerns has further restricted the governmental initiative in pioneering through its own instrumentalities the research and developmental work which has constituted the major portion of nuclear-energy programs elsewhere. The nationalization of the electricity industry in 1962 will inevitably open the way to more participation of state agencies in nuclear reactor development.[23]

The efforts to establish a specialized nuclear-energy agency in Italy culminated in the bill of 1960, which conferred a permanent legal status on the National Committee for Nuclear Energy (Comitato Nazionale per l'Energia Nucleare), but restricted its functions to general oversight of the various aspects of the program, particularly the technical-regulatory side. In the course of the discussions held before the Senate Commission for Industry, it was made clear that the committee should have neither executive nor administrative tasks already held by existing departments. In the final text, the original authority to delegate such tasks to the committee was abandoned, leaving the committee with the difficult problem of asserting such influence as it could to co-ordinate the work of various departments already in the field.

The general programs and policies of the National Committee are laid down by a ministerial group consisting of the prime minister and the ministers of Foreign Affairs, the Treasury, Industry and Commerce, and Education, with other ministers able to participate when their interests are involved.

The National Committee for Nuclear Energy is closely identified with one particular department for all operating purposes —the Ministry of Industry and Commerce. The minister of this department is not only a key member of the interministerial policy group, but is also chairman of the governing board of the National Committee. In this position he is able, paradoxically, to report on behalf of the committee (as chairman) to himself (as the minister responsible for the work of the committee). The managerial board, in addition to the minister of industry and commerce as chairman, consists of a number of members chosen from experts in nuclear science and its technical or commercial applications. The directors-general of the Ministry of Industry and Commerce and the Ministry of Education are also members of the managing board.

---

[23] The newly created National Board for Electric Energy (Ente Nazionale per l'Energia Elettrica) is to take over the whole electricity industry, which means that nuclear-generating plants will be state owned and operated.

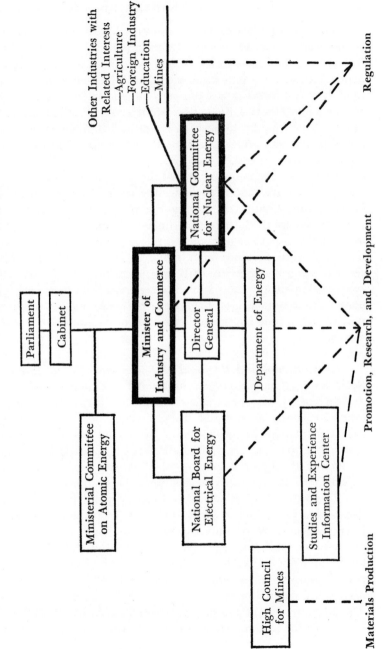

FIG. 6. ATOMIC-ENERGY ORGANIZATION IN ITALY

The only specialized agency concerned with nuclear energy is the Studies and Experience Information Center (Centro Informazioni Studi Esperienze), created in 1945 on the initiative of Milan industrialists and some scientists. The center was subsequently transformed into a company supported in part by such private industries as Edison, Fiat, Montecatini, Pirelli, and Sade and by several public authorities. It has contributed to the training of personnel in nuclear science and technology and in fostering research in general.

In essence, the major aspects of the government's nuclear-energy program are conducted under the aegis of the Ministry of Industry and Commerce, leaving the National Committee for Nuclear Science in the role of technical advisor on such matters as the safety of nuclear reactors and power plants and on the various regulations covering other radiation hazards. The committee also sponsors research with its own funds and is actively concerned with all international agreements on nuclear-energy matters. At this stage, it is obviously an extremely modest counterpart to the atomic energy authorities of other countries in this survey.

International and Regional Organizations. At the international level a number of organizations and structures to deal with nuclear energy have been created. Some are intergovernmental, others are non-governmental; they include world-wide and regional permanent organizations as well as *ad hoc* conferences. Their programs may embrace a full spectrum of activities or may be limited to one or more aspects. They are so numerous and varied that only a selective description is possible here.

The only organization with substantially universal membership and a full range of programs is the International Atomic Energy Agency. Its structure is generally similar to that of many of the other specialized agencies making up the United Nations family and not unlike the nuclear organizations created in the participating states. A general conference at which all members may be represented meets annually for about two weeks to make decisions on some of the principal problems facing the agency. Typical of the matters settled are the admission of new members or the decision to enter a relationship agreement with another specialized agency. The conference confirms the board of governors' decisions on the program and recommends new programs.

Responsibility for carrying out the statutory functions of the agency rests on the board of governors. The board meets several times a year and presently consists of twenty-three members selected as closely as political circumstances will permit on the current nuclear capabilities and interests of the principal countries and regions of the world. Proposals relating to the general program are formulated for presentation to the general conference, and the execution of the program under the direction of the secretariat is kept under close and detailed review by the board. An annual report on the activities of the agency is presented to the general conference.

The secretariat of the agency, the third organ specifically provided for in the founding statute, is headed by a director general appointed by the board with the approval of the general conference. The secretariat carries out the program of the agency within the revenues approved in the annual budget and in accordance with decisions and regulations of the board of governors. The director general makes a bimonthly report to the board on all developments affecting the agency and presents miscellaneous reports and proposals to board meetings, as well as drafting board reports for the general conference.

Like its national counterparts, the agency has found it useful to create a Scientific Advisory Committee consisting of seven distinguished scientists each serving in his individual capacity but selected from the leading member states of the agency. The committee advises the board and the director general on proposals or technical programs and projects submitted to it for consideration.

The agency faces the same problem as any of the domestic atomic-energy authorities: its jurisdiction cuts across the fields of interest assigned to other specialized organs of the United Nations and some of the areas covered by regional organizations. There is, consequently, a particular need for establishing co-ordinating devices.

The personnel and financing problems of the agency display features which are not present in national atomic-energy organizations. Staff is selected by the director general, but, for the appointment and dismissal of key officials or those in the politically sensitive Inspection Division, the board must be formally consulted. The merit principle of selection is applied, although it has to be modified to meet the need for geographical distribution of professional staff, which reflects, at least approximately, the contributions made to the agency by various regions of the world. This distribution is insisted on by many states, even though members of the staff become, for the period of their engagement, international civil servants not subject to direction by national governments. Scientists on staff are usually retained for two years; administrators have longer tenures and may even be placed on permanent contract.

In budgetary matters, the agency suffers more from uncertainty about its source of funds than from the inflexibility of the annual appropriation cycle. The reliance on annual appropriations for programs that by their nature usually require several years to complete is clearly embarrassing to the agency. The unfortunate effects of this short-term planning have been somewhat mitigated by adopting a two-year term for research contracts as well as for technical assistance. An appraisal every five years of all the planned activities of the specialized agencies, recently instituted by the Economic and Social Council, does not have the force of a budgetary allocation, but still tends toward more effective forecasting of revenue requirements.

The element of uncertainty in financing the agency stems from the fact that roughly one-quarter of the budget is financed from voluntary contributions made *during* the budget year by the member states. Because the total donations cannot be predicted, it is difficult to plan for these activities except as the money flows in.

Formulation of the annual budget is a lengthy procedure. The director general prepares a preliminary report in the spring of the calendar year preceding the one for which the budget is being drawn. The technical portion of the proposed program may be submitted to the Scientific Advisory Committee for consideration. After preliminary scrutiny of the draft budget by a special committee of the board, the board considers and approves the final budgetary submission for presentation to the annual meeting of the general conference in September. A two-thirds vote of the conference is required for approval, and, although the conference may not change the budget, the budget can be returned to the board with recommendations. Thus far, however, the conference has always approved the budget in the form submitted to it by the board. As a final step, the budgetary committee of the United Nations reports to the General Assembly on the agency's budget, the report being confined to administrative questions.

Supporting and supplementing the work of the International Atomic Energy Agency are a number of regional organizations for which there is space to provide only the briefest organizational description.

The Organization of American States has established an Inter-American Nuclear Energy Commission which does not have a fully independent legal personality but uses the Pan American Union as its secretariat. By the terms of its statute (which was adopted as a resolution of the OAS Council and was not submitted to its member states for signature or ratification), the commission may be converted into a specialized organization and endowed with its own legal personality and a separate secretariat. Designed broadly to facilitate co-operation among the member states in matters relating to peaceful applications of nuclear energy, it is specifically directed to assist the American republics in developing research and training plans, exchanging scientific and technical information, developing public health measures, and studying and recommending measures for achieving these ends.

The European Nuclear Energy Agency was established as an adjunct to OEEC (now the Organization for European Co-operation and Development) by a decision of the council. The agency does not have independent legal personality, and its secretariat forms part of the secretariat of the parent organization. Its Steering Committee carries out the assigned functions, reserving political or structural questions for the Council of OECD. The agency has a number of co-ordinating responsibili-

ties designed to harmonize national programs, foster joint undertakings for the production and use of nuclear energy, promote
agreements for the supply of nuclear materials to the member
states, examine measures for the greatest possible freedom of international trade in this field, establish (through the Security
Control Convention) safeguards for the activities which it assists, and to generally harmonize national legislation relating to
nuclear energy.

EURATOM is a supragovernmental organization of the
European communities, comparable to the European Common
Market and the European Coal and Steel Community. It was
created by international treaty and has an autonomous legal personality. However, it shares with the other two organizations the
Parliament and Court of Justice, as well as using, with the Common Market, the Economic and Social Committee. Like the
other organizations, it deals with a full spectrum of nuclear-
energy activities, including research, dissemination of information, health protection, establishment of joint enterprises, creation of a supply organization and a nuclear common market,
and the exercise of safeguards. Several of these functions are supported by a provision that the community is to own all fissionable material in the territory of its members, except that reserved for military purposes.

The special attribute which sets EURATOM apart from
other international organizations is that it may make decisions
that are directly binding on the member states. Furthermore,
such decisions do not need to be reached unanimously on the
basis of equal voting power; voting strength is related to a
formula, established by treaty, which is based on each country's
contribution to the community.

Other regional organizations have been created to handle
a more limited range of activities associated with the peaceful
uses of atomic energy. The European Council for Nuclear Research (CERN) is, for most practical purposes, a type of corporation to which member states make contributions in accordance
with a scale annexed to the founding treaty, but in which they
all have equal votes. The specific program is laid down in the

treaty, and participants are not required to contribute to any activities not specified by the treaty. The Joint Institute for Nuclear Research (JINR) is eastern Europe's counterpart to CERN, established and organized in a similar fashion for the same purposes.

Belgium is the seat of EUROCHEMIC, an undertaking of the European Nuclear Energy Agency, established by an international convention as a joint stock company. In part it is governed by both international law and its own covenant and statute and in part by Belgium law. The shares of the company were allocated to the governments or to the nuclear-energy authorities of the participating states. EUROCHEMIC has clearly delimited functions: constructing and operating a plant and laboratory for processing irradiated fuels from reactors in the member states and training specialists in this field.

In addition to the foregoing international organizations, a number of joint programs or projects have been established to enable states, nuclear-energy institutes, and international organizations to participate in various ways. Thus, JENER is a co-operative Norwegian-Dutch program for operating the JEEP reactor. A joint commission (three members from each country) administers the program, the facilities being owned by the Norwegian Atomic Energy Institute. Similarly, the HALDEN Reactor Project, organized under the European Nuclear Energy Agency, involves Norway, Austria, Denmark, Sweden, the United Kingdom, Switzerland and EURATOM. A committee representing each of the participants draws up the program, and an international team of scientists and technicians employed by the Norwegian Institute carries out the program. The original agreement was signed for three years, but it has since been extended to eighteen months, with provision for a further wind up period of another twelve months. The European Nuclear Energy Agency, as the sponsoring body, is represented at the meetings of the HALDEN Committee and also participates in the work of the secretariat to the project. The same group of states also participates in the DRAGON Project, which is organized on almost an identical basis, except that the United Kingdom Atomic

Energy Authority owns and operates the reactor. The project is staffed by an international team seconded from the participating states or from ENEA.

This outline of the organizations for handling the peaceful uses of atomic energy reveals a number of common administrative problems which can be most fruitfully explored by examining each element of the program—a task to which the next three chapters of this study are devoted.

IV
Provision of
Nuclear Materials

The term "nuclear materials" used in this chapter requires elaboration before the administrative problems arising in connection with the provision or procurement of such materials can be discussed. There are three components involved. First, there is the raw material itself, frequently referred to as "source material": this consists of uranium, thorium, and the other natural minerals from which the fissionable isotopes uranium 235, 233, and 234 and the artificially produced element plutonium are extracted. Second, these isotopes of uranium, as well as the element plutonium, are defined by most jurisdictions as "special nuclear material" or "fissionable material." Finally, there is the by-product material which is derived from nuclear fission or made radioactive by exposure to the fissioning material. The by-product material in the form of radioactive isotopes has a variety of applications already briefly described in the introductory chapter.

The source material is susceptible to all the mining and processing techniques which enter into the production of more conventional ores, coupled with fabrication procedures designed to prepare the metal for fueling reactors. If source material could not be directed to warlike purposes, there would be no reason to impose special controls on its use, different from the standard controls imposed on other mining, processing, and fabricating activities. The special nuclear materials, as well as the by-product materials, on the other hand, are not raw materials but are the end products of expensive and hazardous processes which have been deemed by all countries to raise such special problems that very rigorous regulation, if not outright state monopoly of the materials, has been involved. In a sense special nuclear materials used, for example, to fuel a reactor employing enriched uranium are the raw materials for such productive purposes; but this does not alter the fact that they must be subjected to more rigorous control than is required for the source materials out of which they are produced.

With these distinctions in mind, we are now in a position to examine the way in which each country has grappled with the production or procurement of the essential ingredients for its atomic-energy programs. Only two of the six countries under examination, Canada and Japan, have seen fit to create special organizations to deal with the provision of nuclear materials. The others rely on the central atomic-energy authorities to arrange for the provision of such materials. This organizational difference cannot be accounted for simply on the grounds that these two countries have such large domestic supplies of the source material that no other option was open to them. Although it is true that Canada is the world's second largest producer of uranium, the United States and France are also important producers, and Japan imports most of its source material. The time lag in initiating a program in Japan, accompanied by the urge to achieve self-sufficiency in special nuclear materials, probably accounts for the decision taken by that country to supplement its central atomic-energy authority with a separate Atomic Fuel Corporation. In Canada, the relevant factors are more complex, and, since this country's problems in the production field have probably been the most acute, the Canadian experience is worth more extended attention.

During the war, Canada became the prime supplier of the source materials required by her beleaguered allies and, in particular, by the Manhattan Project which was working on the atom bomb in the United States. This commitment was met by reopening in 1942 an abandoned radium mine, originally incorporated under private ownership in 1927 as Eldorado Gold Mines Ltd. In January, 1944, the government expropriated the mine and bought out the private shareholders. A year later, the transition was completed by converting the enterprise into a Crown company called Eldorado Mining and Refining Ltd.[1]

Under its founding order in council, Eldorado was entrusted with responsibility for exploration, development, and operation of mineral properties and the production, refining, sale, or disposal of radium and other products. In September, 1943, even before the incorporation of Eldorado, the government signified its intention of conferring a monopoly on the Crown by reserving to it all new discoveries of radioactive minerals in the Yukon and Northwest territories and by prohibiting private participation, even in prospecting. This policy persisted until 1948, when private industry was invited to enter the field.[2] As a consequence, in the initial stages, Eldorado accounted for the first major discoveries and mining developments and in conjunction with other federal departments—notably the Mines Branch of the Department of Mines and Technical Surveys—pioneered new processes. It was not until 1953 that private industry began to make a significant contribution to the production of uranium and, indeed, shortly outstripped the government-operated mines and plants. Unfortunately, at a time when these new mines were coming into full production, gloomy forecasts of world demand for uranium, coupled with increased production elsewhere, dimmed the glowing prospects which had encouraged an old-fashioned mining boom among Canadian prospectors and mining interests.

These private concerns were at least formally beyond the jurisdiction of Eldorado Mining and Refining, for their exploration and mining permits were granted by another agency, the Atomic Energy Control Board. However, by virtue of its position as the sole purchaser of uranium ore and operator of the only uranium refinery in Canada, the company became the

---

[1] The fullest account of developments in source materials is found in W. D. G. Hunter, "The Development of the Canadian Uranium Industry: An Experiment in Public Enterprise," *The Canadian Journal of Economics and Political Science*, XXVIII (August 1962), 329–352.

[2] It should be noted that the federal government's writ runs only in the territories; consequently, to first enforce the government monopoly and then to withdraw it required action by each of the provinces in which claims had been staked.

government's chief instrument for coping with the crisis. Company purchases were made on the basis of special price contracts with private producers. These contracts were adjusted several times to foster production, particularly from low-grade ores. The terms were primarily based on agreements with the United States Atomic Energy Commission, Eldorado's sole customer until quite recently; they called for delivery by the company of specific quantities at certain prices, and it was through these agreements that the company sought to co-ordinate and ultimately to taper off production by private plants. In August, 1955, the government announced that after March 31, 1956, no further special contracts would be negotiated by Eldorado with private producers. This pronouncement anticipated by two years the announcement of the United States authorities in November, 1958, that they were not prepared to take up their options to purchase Canadian uranium after 1963. The decision was a great blow to Canadian producers who, looking at previous wartime demands and the continuing inability to achieve international agreement on control over military uses, had been deluded into thinking that there would be an ever expanding demand for uranium. But continuing international tension had encouraged the United States to embark actively on a program of its own to ensure sufficient domestic resources, and, by 1956, this initiative had resulted in a plentiful stock of uranium. Other countries were equally engaged in boosting production of source materials. Even as world production was thus mounting, the first estimates of world requirements for uranium, especially in its application to the production of power, were shown to have been inflated by optimistic forecasts of the short time it would take to produce atomic power at competitive prices. Conventional sources of energy, like coal and oil, have not declined as expected, and the great future held out for nuclear-generated power has been projected into the 1970's.

Although the crisis of overproduction was not really of the Canadian government's making, its position as the monopolist purchaser of uranium compelled it to take action, particularly because no genuine private market existed in which the normal forces of supply and demand could be allowed to have free play.

Accordingly, the government sought to cushion the shock to the Canadian uranium industry by formulating a "stretch-out" delivery program and a phased shutdown of mines, extending to 1965. Eldorado had the administrative means to implement this program; it was responsible for allocating production quotas to the various mining interests, many of which merged to get maximum benefits. This was a somewhat invidious responsibility because Eldorado has mining ventures of its own to consider in devising the allocations.

Supplementing this phased program for tapering off production, research has been channeled into new industrial applications for uranium in an effort to create new markets. This work has been guided by Atomic Energy of Canada through its own facilities and through encouragement to private industry and other government departments engaged in research. The assumption is that, if the industry can be tided over the doldrum period, renewed demand for uranium to fuel the power reactors expected to become economically feasible in the next decade will provide a fresh impetus to lagging uranium sales. In the interval, acute dislocation of the communities which have mushroomed around uranium-mining sites has involved both federal and provincial authorities in complex salvaging operations.

Presumably, as long as the future remains uncertain, the government, working through Eldorado Mining and Refining, will not be able to retreat from its responsibilities in the field of nuclear source materials. Its direct mining commitments would, however, appear to be purely a wartime emergency development. The company has already abandoned exploration of further mining prospects, and one of its major ore bodies has been exhausted and the mine closed down. There would now appear to be no urgent reason for the government to retain its operational role in the mining field.

Similarly, Eldorado's position as the sole purchaser and seller of uranium has had to be abandoned. The oversupply of uranium enabled the government in May, 1958, to give private producers the right to market their uranium under export licenses granted by the Atomic Energy Control Board and the

Department of Trade and Commerce. However, Eldorado still retains responsibility for ensuring that all obligations under the supply contracts are satisfied. In addition, since emphasis is placed on exporting only the pure product and since Eldorado still operates the only refinery plant, the monopolistic position remains very strong. Until 1955, the refinery could produce only uranium black oxide which had to be sent to the Atomic Energy Commission of the United States for further purification before it could be used in the various atomic-energy installations. In mid-1955, new refining techniques, which were developed by Eldorado's own research division and which made possible the production of the purified form of nuclear grade orange oxide used in making uranium metal, went into operation. Subsequently, in April, 1958, after further research and pilot plant operations, the company began to produce its own metal on a commercial scale. Actual fabrication of the uranium metal rods for use in reactors is, however, now in the hands of private companies.

The direct involvement of Eldorado in all phases of the uranium production cycle necessitated the creation of a special research and development division in 1953. This division covers the whole spectrum from mine ore to metal fabrication, maintaining close working relations with producers, the Mines Branch, other research establishments in universities, Atomic Energy of Canada and, abroad, with the atomic-energy authorities of the United States and Britain.

As in the case of mining the ore itself, the present monopoly of the refining business needs careful reconsideration. Other countries are able to maintain effective control over source materials without conferring a monopoly on a government agency. A transfer of the government's refining activities to private enterprise would then permit a corresponding transfer of the research aspects of the work to existing agencies such as Atomic Energy of Canada Ltd. and the Department of Mines and Technical Surveys. In short, the time may be ripe to contemplate winding up Eldorado Mining and Refining Ltd. and transferring its mining and refining activities to private concerns and its research and sales divisions to other departments and agencies. No

loss of necessary controls would result from government withdrawal in these fields.[3]

This lengthy assessment of one country's efforts to cope with
the problems of administering the source materials required for
an atomic-energy program may serve as the prototype for other
countries faced with the same problems. Canada, as the earliest
and largest producer, has had to grapple with all the difficulties
that are likely to arise in the raw material field, and this detailed account of its experiences permits us to examine in much
briefer compass the developments in other countries. As was
noted earlier, Japan is the only other country of the six under
review to follow the Canadian organizational pattern of creating
a special agency to deal with the production or supply of nuclear source materials. The Atomic Fuel Corporation is the
direct counterpart, in its organizational form and in its wholly
government-controlled capital, to Canada's Eldorado Mining
and Refining Company. It occupies the third tier in the organizational complex which administers Japan's nuclear-energy program, subordinate to both the Atomic Energy Bureau and the
top-ranking Atomic Energy Commission.

The exploration and mining aspects of the production
cycle, though under the direct supervision of the Atomic Fuel
Corporation, have not been as important as in Canada, primarily
because Japan's natural uranium resources can be exploited
only at relatively high cost. When prospecting first began in
1957, it was commonly believed that uranium was a scarce com-
modity, but the developments already outlined quickly dispelled
this impression. As a result, in the period from 1957 to 1960,
budgeted expenditures for prospecting were cut in half while
there was over a fourfold increase in allocations for the purchase
of nuclear materials. The corporation has, accordingly, restricted

---

[3] One is tempted to speculate that the original decision to provide a separate organization for handling nuclear materials in Canada was made possible by the fact that the research and development side of the program
relied entirely on natural uranium. In other countries, special nuclear materials were not only needed for, but were actually produced by, research and
development; consequently, it may have made more administrative sense to
combine all aspects of materials procurement, whether source or special
materials, with the agency also concerned with research and promotion.

itself to tests of mining and milling on a modest scale. Despite subsidies paid to sixty-two mining interests to encourage private prospecting, the results have not been particularly rewarding.

At this early stage of development in Japan, the corporation's attention is directed primarily to refining and to the possibility of enriching uranium and reprocessing spent fuels. The future of refining operations depends to some extent on the particular technology to be employed in reactor development. If the trend is toward reactors charged with natural uranium—a technology which Canadian government scientists, for example, are disposed to think holds the key to success in power reactor development—then possibly a sufficiently large commerical basis to sustain a private refining industry can be contemplated. On the other hand, if the future lies with enriched uranium fuel, as several of the major members of the nuclear club maintain, then the prospects for private industry are less promising. The enrichment of uranium and the reprocessing of spent fuels are still very much at the research and developmental stages, but it is likely that the Atomic Fuel Corporation would be required to operate such plants in the event that future developments warrant their construction. The fabrication of fuel elements, perhaps the most immediate next step in Japan's program, can, undoubtedly, as in other countries, be undertaken by private enterprise. Clearly, the major operational tasks for the Atomic Fuel Corporation lie in the future, and, as long as an official policy of seeking to achieve a self-sufficient nuclear-energy program is maintained, there will be an expanding field of endeavor for the corporation.

In the United Kingdom, no significant deposits of uranium have been found, and, in any event, the increasing world supply at reduced costs has not provided much incentive to embark on an active program of domestic exploration. Consequently, Britain has not faced anything like the problems which Canada faces as one of the largest producers of source material. Essentially, all that was required was some machinery to ensure the procurement of the necessary source materials. This function has been undertaken for Britain by the Combined Development Agency, a joint body representing Canada, the United States, and the United Kingdom. The extreme shortage of uranium in the early years necessitated the formation of this agency to allocate uranium supplies and, in particular, to ensure Britain an adequate quantity of source material from areas outside Canada and the United States—notably the Congo, Portugal, South Africa, and Australia. In 1956, some of Canada's uranium as well was diverted from the United States to the United Kingdom. Responsibility for arranging purchases of source material through the Combined Development Agency is carried by the central London office of the United Kingdom Atomic Energy Authority. The closing down of the Combined Development Agency in 1962 left the London office to negotiate contracts with producers like Canada.

The government monopoly of procurement of source materials is extended to the provision of special nuclear materials as well. The authority's Operations Group is in charge of the processing of uranium and of metal-fabrication. Similarly, fuel elements for power reactors and enriched uranium fuel are manufactured in plants operated by the authority. The largest commercial revenues come from the authority's sales of fuel elements, and the future prospects are most promising, provided that the United Kingdom can induce other countries to adopt its reactors—as both the Italian and Japanese governments are now partially committed to do.

Thus far, British developments have been characterized by centralized government procurement of nuclear source material and the Production Group's virtual monopoly of all processing and manufacturing procedures required to produce the special nuclear materials for the authority. Thus, the authority is in a strong position to regulate the entire development with respect to the peaceful uses of atomic energy, particularly its industrial applications. In Britain, the speed and freedom with which atomic energy can be exploited by private business for commercial use depend very largely on decisions and actions taken by the authority with respect to relinquishing some of its hold over the nuclear materials themselves. There is little indication at present that it is willing, or that government policy will permit it, to surrender its dominant role.

In the United States, a rather different situation has developed in the production of nuclear materials. From the beginning, prospecting and mining have been left in private hands. The nuclear source material required for the military development of the atomic bomb was provided, as previously indicated, by Canada. But the prolongation of the Cold War and the desire to ensure adequate supplies induced the Atomic Energy Commission to foster domestic exploration and mining. By 1956, more than nine hundred mines were in operation, and the United States had become the world's largest producer of source materials. It was as a follow-up to this development and in view of the mounting oversupply of uranium stocks throughout the world that the United States government took the decision, which had the adverse consequences already mentioned, to curtail its purchases from Canada.

Whereas prospecting and production were freely undertaken by private interests, all purchases were made by the Atomic Energy Commission under guaranteed price arrangements. Furthermore, the commission was empowered by the Atomic Energy Act of 1954 to seize, condemn, or otherwise acquire any stocks of source materials; the commission was also authorized to take over lands which were not being worked but which were considered worthy of exploration for the uranium deposits they contained. Once removed from the soil, all source material is subject to specific licensing requirements imposed by the Atomic Energy Commission.

Again, quite unlike the situation in other countries, the further processing, refining, and fabrication of ores to produce special nuclear materials are conducted to a large extent in private establishments. Even the operation of nuclear reactors by private firms became possible after the Act of 1954 permitted the commission to release sufficient special nuclear materials to make privately operated reactors feasible. However, not only do all these activities have to be performed under strict licensing arrangements, but all rights, title, and interest in special nuclear materials remain the property of the United States.

In short, although strict control over all nuclear materials is imposed by the Atomic Energy Commission, the operations

connected with the production of both source and special nuclear materials are much more in private hands than is true of
any of the other countries included in this survey. Nevertheless,
the government monopoly of special nuclear materials still per-
sists despite strong agitation to abandon it at the time that the
Atomic Energy Act was being amended in 1954. Congress insisted, "It is essential to the common defense and security that
title to all special nuclear material be in the United States, while
such material is within the United States." [4] Thus, although
private firms or individuals participate in the production process,
they retain no rights over the special materials they employ and
are required to sell the products to the commission.

France's efforts to bring her nuclear-energy program into
being were frustrated by an initial lack of source materials; a
tiny supply of uranium cached in Morocco and some heavy
water spirited away to Norway at the beginning of the war
constituted the only source of supply until the first local deposits were discovered in France in 1948 by the Atomic Energy
Authority's own prospectors. Although there has never been any
prohibition against private undertakings in this sphere, the early
stages of all intensive prospecting both in France and in the
French overseas domains were undertaken by the authority. In
1954, a more positive policy to stimulate private enterprise to
enter the field was adopted, with the result that about one-fifth
of the uranium concentrate now comes from private producers,
and France has become the world's fourth largest uranium producer.

The French Atomic Energy Authority also took the lead in
setting up plants for processing the ore. Treatment plants are
operated by the authority as mixed private and public undertakings in which the authority holds a substantial investment.
This pattern of direct operation, contracts with private firms, or
the use of special companies with mixed government and private
participation characterizes the whole field of production of the
special nuclear materials. Although no statutory provisions cover
the production or transfer of such materials, in practice the
Atomic Energy Authority effectively monopolizes the products,

[4] Quoted in Kruse, *op. cit.*, p. 50.

and they are "in no way objects of commercial transactions." [5] Source materials in the hands of private owners are produced under strict licensing arrangements, and although they do not have to be sold to the authority, that agency's position is reinforced by its power to expropriate such materials—a power which it has not, so far, had to use.

The recent adoption of detailed atomic-energy legislation in Italy clarifies the present situation with respect to administering the nuclear materials side of the program. The treaty of the European Atomic Community (EURATOM) leaves the member states free to devise their own methods for dealing with source materials. In Italy, the Mines Law is expected to extend to uranium like any other mineral. This means that exploration and mining by private entrepreneurs take place under a state licensing system, and ownership of the minerals resides in the state. All domestic and foreign trade in any nuclear substance is similarly governed by licenses and permits. In any event, most of the special nuclear materials have been procured by Italy on the basis of international or bilateral agreements which prescribe rigorous conditions for the recipient country. In much the same fashion, the international and regional nuclear-energy agencies described in the previous chapter procure their nuclear supplies by donations from participating members, normally reserving to the member states such nuclear material as they require for their domestic military applications.

Among the countries surveyed, there is considerable variation in the methods used to handle the nuclear materials involved in their respective atomic-energy programs. In all countries, the special nuclear materials are subjected to particularly rigorous controls, for the most part by placing the atomic-energy authority in the position of monopolist purchaser and by retaining the state's legal title to the materials or giving it powers

---

[5] *Ibid.*, p. 52. French antipathy to regulation of nuclear source materials is explained by one official of the Atomic Energy Authority on the grounds that "the abundance of this mineral throughout the world is such that a policy of safeguards encourages countries anxious to preserve their independence to produce their own uranium. This inevitably had led to an increase in general production, harming the interests of future world-wide nuclear disarmament" (Goldschmidt, *op. cit.*, p. 41).

of expropriation. This situation prevails even where, as in the United States, private enterprise has been enlisted in the production program. Nuclear source materials do not raise problems of the same magnitude, but even here, with opportunities for wider private participation, all activities are carried out under strict systems of licensing and permits. Indeed, in the United Kingdom, a virtual government monopoly over the procurement of raw materials prevails; in Canada, the initial government monopoly is only now beginning to be abandoned; and everywhere, international trade in these substances is governed by intergovernmental agreements which eliminate the normal workings of the free market. Quite apart from the critical economic issues posed for the large producers of nuclear materials, it is evident that the basic administrative problem is one of devising proper controls. The monopolistic or quasi-monopolistic position of the state is not merely a by-product of the initial efforts to ensure supplies for the military effort, but also enables the state, for safety and security reasons, to know who has the material or where and to whom it is being sold. These considerations also account for the essentially intergovernmental nature of all transactions abroad, for most of the traffic in nuclear materials of all kinds is between a state production or procurement agency and an atomic-energy agency of the recipient country.

V
Research and Development

Apart from the countries which are important producers of nuclear source materials, the hard core of operations in the atomic-energy program consists of research and development. Some of these activities are associated with the production of source materials and more particularly with the provision of special nuclear materials. Research on radioactive isotopes—their production and application to a wide range of experimental, industrial, and medical uses—constitutes another important element of the program from which modest revenues are now being earned by some countries. But the most massive research and developmental efforts have been directed to devising the most efficient techniques for generating nuclear energy and to applying this new source of energy in various ways once it has been activated.

In all these operations, the state itself has had to take a much more active part than has characteristically been the case in exploiting other forms of energy. Beginning with a wartime situation which necessitated the rapid assembling of men and resources possible only through direct governmental involvement, the initiative still remains very much in the hands of the state. The research spectrum is so broad that an unprecedented variety of scientific and technical disciplines has had to be brought to bear on both the basic and applied sides. In some instances, new disciplines have even emerged, with a consequent need to provide continuous training programs which the universities, as the traditional sources of supply of scientific manpower, were not immediately equipped to provide. In addition, research and development in the nuclear-energy field have had to nourish each other in an unprecedented fashion: the two aspects of the program have had to be executed simultaneously without the usual time lag between pure research, its experimental application in prototypes, and its ultimate commercial application. In a very real sense, a commercial nuclear power plant today still remains a vast laboratory from which researchers obtain fresh data to be fed back through the draftsmen and engineers to improve the design and construction of new plants. Similarly, a fresh appreciation of the economics of nuclear power production may bring forth a new requirement for a plant capable of substantially greater production than was originally deemed necessary; the new appraisal, as a result, throws the problem back into the laboratories and design rooms.[1]

The difficulty of separating these various elements and, particularly, of establishing a clear dividing line between development and commercial applications suggests the merit of combining these closely related activities for purposes of description and analysis. The magnitude and cost of these operations, together with the risk and uncertainty attending their commercial application, have brought about a close partnership between government and private undertakings which further underlines the value of examining all these operations together. Overriding all these considerations and regardless of whether state or private firms are conducting the research and development are the hazards to the health and safety of the workers and the community at large in the performance of all these operations. Regulation by state instrumentality is, therefore, an inescapable responsibility which cannot be devolved to non-governmental bodies.

For research and development, we confront a situation in which the state has assumed a dominant operational and regulatory role and in which a high degree of concentration into one state authority has taken place. In all countries, collaboration with private industry and the universities has been sought, but

---

[1] For an illustration of the planning problems raised by such reassessments, see *The Economist*, October 27, 1962, pp. 380–381.

it is a collaboration that leaves the state with the lion's share of the actual conduct of research as well as of the subsequent practical applications to which the research findings may be put. The question remains: What is the role of the non-state agencies, and what should be their relations with the central government organs vested with over-all responsibility for the nuclear-energy program?

The answer, as the experience of the countries surveyed demonstrates, is dependent on the degree of maturity attained by the universities and the state of the scientific and technical arts in each nation. In the more advanced countries, notably in the United States, the central atomic-energy agency has been able to lean heavily on highly developed scientific and industrial establishments, as well as drawing on the resources of the universities, not only for the developmental aspects, but also for the research portions of the program. France, the United Kingdom, and Canada have had to rely much more on governmental resources although, as the initial concentration of state effort begins to pay off, more and more efforts are being made to encourage the use of private resources and skills. Japan's need to import its technology and build from the ground up the necessary skills and resources leaves no question but that the state will continue to occupy the center of the stage and that the private sector will for some time continue to occupy a peripheral place. In the directed economies of other nations, where completely state-owned systems are axiomatic, or in underdeveloped nations, the problem of delimiting the respective roles of the state and the private participants is, of course, rather academic.

The bearing of these general observations on the specific experience of each of the countries surveyed is worthy of detailed comment, and it will be appropriate to begin with the United States.

The United States. The Atomic Energy Commission currently spends over $2,500,000,000 to carry out all its promotional, operating, and regulatory responsibilities. Close to three-quarters of this amount is devoted to the procurement of source materials, the production of fissionable materials, and the weapons program. Though weapons research and production obviously continue to absorb the bulk of the budget, research and development activities directed toward peaceful applications have been steadily growing.

The laboratory research installations of the commission were erected to accomplish certain specific missions generally oriented toward large-scale projects such as nuclear-powered aircraft and rockets, civilian power reactors, naval propulsion reactors, and weapons development. These direct research commitments were and continue to be supplemented increasingly by a wide range of research contracts and grants designed to encourage the fullest use of the research capabilities of universities and private industries.

Such grants and contracts for research are by no means unique; they have been standard methods by which the federal government has financed research for many years. These methods have brought to the fore and accentuated a number of perplexing problems inherent in the intervention of science in government and government in science. No one discounts the benefits to government, industry, and the universities (including individual researchers). But problems do exist. Which, for example, is the best way of financing research—the contract or the grant? How far should the universities themselves sponsor research in this field over and above that financed by government funds? Is federal support of research in certain fields, such as nuclear physics, likely to distort the total research programs of universities? Once support on this scale is given, how can it be withdrawn or redirected to other programs? Is the government properly equipped to evaluate the research proposals originating in universities with a view to establishing priorities or to assessing the quality of the results? Is there not a problem when the same people who may be recipients of contracts are also members of the committees which evaluate proposed projects?

Both the Atomic Energy Commission and the universities are well aware of these problems, even though general formulas for solving them have thus far proved elusive. For the government itself, perhaps the major unresolved problem relates to the future of the commission's own laboratories. Dr. Alvin M. Weinberg, research director of Oak Ridge National Laboratory, has noted that the technical problems which gave rise to the project-oriented laboratories have "finite dimensions."

> It is therefore unlikely [he concludes] that the problems big enough to challenge big laboratories will continue to be in the areas of technology for which the laboratories were originally organized . . . the institutions must inevitably be prepared to move into areas outside their original interests if they are to retain immortality.[2]

Obsolescence or redundancy produced by scientific success is likely to be an equally important problem for other countries where the governmental research installations are specially created to meet the needs of the atomic-energy program. The future of such laboratories clearly rests in finding new problems with dimensions of the same order as those which confronted the researchers in the pioneering stages of nuclear-energy development. These are most likely to be found in an area that encompasses more than the field of nuclear energy—perhaps one directed more generally to energy resources or natural resources as a whole.

The urgency which characterized the wartime stage in the development of nuclear energy necessitated a crash program of staff training. For reasons of security and secrecy, most nuclear establishments were set up in remote sites, and at first training was very much an *ad hoc,* on-the-job arrangement. With the increase in knowledge and an almost explosive growth in staff, more formal arrangements had to be made, and, in the main, the burden of providing instruction fell on the national laboratories such as Argonne and Oak Ridge.[3] Not only was it necessary to provide special courses for staff within the laboratories, but staff of private concerns and universities to whom contract assignments had been given also had to be instructed. Training was concentrated primarily on nuclear power technology and on the application of radioactive isotopes.

---

[2] Alvin M. Weinberg, "Future Aims of Large Scale Research," *Chemical and Engineering News,* XLVII (1955), 2188–2189.

[3] See the useful discussions in *Education and Nuclear Energy,* report on a seminar held July 6–10, 1959, jointly sponsored by UNESCO and the International Atomic Energy Agency (Vienna: IAEA, 1960), pp. 31–32.

The proliferation of knowledge about the theoretical and applied aspects of nuclear technology reduced the importance of security considerations and thereby opened the door to wider university participation in instruction. New courses in nuclear science and engineering were offered by a number of universities with a consequent cutback in the training programs developed and offered on an emergency basis by the national laboratories. Their instructional courses (which are not full university courses) now are more specific. This interplay between the government laboratories and the universities has had mutually beneficial results. Thus, although the nuclear reactor was largely the brain child of researchers in the national laboratories, the high-energy particle accelerator grew out of university research; universities now have nuclear reactors, and the national laboratories have built accelerators to university designs. Training responsibilities have been correspondingly divided: the national laboratories have undertaken most of the training for nuclear reactors, whereas the universities have concentrated on training with regard to accelerators.

The increasing availability of radioisotopes and their rapidly expanding field of application to a variety of research purposes and industrial uses gave rise to the need for short courses to familiarize the users with the new substances. For a number of reasons, the national laboratories rather than the universities have been the most appropriate agencies for undertaking this training. Isotopes are used by a heterogeneous group representing a great variety of educational backgrounds not easily fitted into the regular departmental structure of universities. A series of short courses is equally unsuited to a university schedule. Finally, the mature person who usually attends such courses finds himself more at home in the environment of the national laboratories. For much the same reasons, the laboratories have been more suited than the universities to providing special instruction for students coming from abroad under the atoms-for-peace program of the United States. These courses, supplemented by visits, seminars, and symposia, represent a distinctive contribution of governmental research centers to education in these specialized branches of science and technology; it is unlikely that these educational activities will be assumed by the universities.

Turning now to the developmental aspects of the United States' nuclear-energy program, we find a similar concern to devolve as much of the operational responsibilities as possible on to private industry and the universities. When it became apparent in 1954 that the peaceful applications, particularly for nuclear-generated power, had immense possibilities, the Atomic Energy Act was amended to enable the commission to permit private firms and individuals to employ the special nuclear materials required. In setting forth its reasons for this change in policy, the commission stated:

> At present, atomic energy is a Government-owned industry. This departure from the normal pattern of industrial enterprise in the country was not taken capriciously or with intent to alter our institutions. It was deemed necessary to cope with the unique and unfamiliar characteristics of atomic energy and because its products then went almost entirely into our military arsenals. Continuance of complete Government dominance into the period of major practical applications, involving as it would a basic change in the fundamental roles of Government and of private individuals and firms, could produce a change in our society as significant in its way as any that might accrue from the technical novelty of nuclear power.
>
> In order that the principal effect of realizing nuclear power may be to confirm and strengthen rather than to change our economic institutions and our way of life, we believe that nuclear power should be produced and distributed by the private and public power systems and not by the Commission.[4]

The immense cost and technical uncertainties of power-reactor development constituted a substantial impediment to the successful implementation of this policy. The Atomic Energy Commission has, consequently, promoted a number of inducements to encourage the broadest private collaboration in the developmental aspects of its program.

In order to demonstrate the technical and operational feasibility of nuclear power reactors, the commission has designed and built a number of experimental reactors. In con-

---

[4] Congress of the United States, *Hearings before the Joint Committee on Atomic Energy*, 83rd Cong., 2nd Sess., S. 3323 and H.R. 8862 (1954), p. 574.

junction with certain publicly owned utilities, the commission has provided the reactor portion of an electrical generating plant, leaving the utility to furnish the conventional equipment and to operate the plant. Finally, research and development assistance from the commission has been used to encourage private companies to build nuclear power plants. In return for these various types of assistance, publicly and privately owned utilities are required to give the Atomic Energy Commission full access to information on all operating and financial results.[5]

The primary purpose of these programs is to enable industry ultimately to construct, without government assistance, power-reactor facilities that will compete on an equal footing with more conventional generating plants. Indeed, the Atomic Energy Act of 1954 (§ 169) specifically prohibits the commission from providing construction or operating subsidies for licensed facilities except in conjunction with a research and development contract.

Progress thus far has been relatively slow. A small number of private installations are under consideration, but only one is in actual operation. In 1962, a combination of sixteen public power authorities in the Pacific Northwest (known as the Washington Public Power Supply System) was authorized by Congress to buy the steam generated by the Hanford plutonium plant, with the prospect of developing 800 MW.[6] In the foreseeable future, federal government investment, particularly in research and development, is likely to play the dominant role. In the long run, as private industry acquires the capacity to assume these new tasks, the declared policy of curtailing and even eliminating the government's stake in these enterprises may ultimately be achieved.

In a country which has anxiously debated the question of public versus private power at least since the halcyon days of the Tennessee Valley Authority in the 1930's, it is not surprising to find a body of opinion that thinks the state should take more

---

[5] Ulysses M. Staebler, "A Summary of Nuclear Power Research and Development in the United States," a paper presented at a conference sponsored by the IAEA in September, 1960, and released as an AEC press release, has a concise discussion of these programs.

[6] For details, see *The Economist*, September 29, 1962, pp. 1194–1196.

active measures to disengage itself from the commercial aspects of the nuclear-power program.[7] Sen. Barry Goldwater voiced this opinion in 1959:

> . . . there was a time when the vehicle used for Government competition and expansion was hydro-electric development, but that time has passed. You now have the atom. That puts the threat of a government power plant in any area, be it Maine or Chicago.[8]

Countering this contention, a former chairman of the Atomic Energy Commission expressed a more realistic view:

> We must all work for a common objective. This is a development job. And now, when we are struggling to formulate rapid and sensible developmental programs, doctrinaire arguments about public versus private power may well jeopardize our progress. Some day this may become an issue—it need not be an issue in the atomic power business now or for years to come. Therefore, speaking for the AEC, I invite the effort and cooperation of everyone.[9]

The co-operative partnership which characterizes the developmental aspects of the nuclear-energy program is maintained by a somewhat unique set of contractual arrangements. The Atomic Energy Commission uses primarily what are known as "integrated contractors," an arrangement by which working capital is provided by the commission, contractor accounts are largely integrated with those of the commission, and the contractor performs the service for a modest management fee or none at all.

This device is not without its problems. Can the commission maintain effective control over planning and administration when the preponderance of technical skills required for such a complex undertaking is mostly in the hands of the contractors? Is there a risk that contractors, by virtue of their close association with the commission, have a preferred access to the plans,

---

[7] For the extreme views held prior to the amended act of 1954, see Kruse, *op. cit.,* p. 30, where the AEC is described as a "Socialist Island" in the economic order.

[8] As quoted in *The New York Times,* "More Work Urged on the Atom," April 8, 1959.

[9] *Loc. cit.*

procedures, and information of that agency, thereby giving them an undue advantage over other firms who may be seeking to gain admission to the nuclear club?

Although these potential drawbacks are inherent in the present relationship between the commission and its associated integrated contractors, there is no evidence that alternative systems are being contemplated. There has been no great pressure to set up a public corporation like those in other countries to undertake these developmental activities. For this reason there has been no attempt to create, following the model of the Tennessee Valley Authority, a public nuclear-power agency to serve as a yardstick against which to measure the performance of private contractors—or, as it is sometimes bluntly put, "to keep them honest."

The United Kingdom. The founding statute of the United Kingdom Atomic Energy Authority (UKAEA), approved in 1954, vested the authority with broad powers to undertake research into "any matters connected with" the production, use, and disposal of atomic energy; the authority itself was empowered to produce, use, and dispose of energy, fissile material, and radioactive substances and could undertake training, educational, and informational activities. Although the authority is permitted to supplement its own research by making contractual arrangements with universities and other institutions including business firms, the greater part of this activity, both in basic and applied fields, continues to be undertaken by the authority in its own research establishments. The Research Group, one of the five groups into which the authority is divided for administrative purposes, is responsible for basic research in atomic physics, including long-term research directed to the controlled release of thermo-nuclear energy and also assists the other groups on special problems.

The Atomic Energy Research Establishment at Harwell is the headquarters for fundamental research, but in June, 1959, the mounting scale of "intramural research" necessitated the opening of a second establishment at Winfreth in Dorset. The principal field stations of the establishment are the Radiochemical Centre at Amersham and the Wantage Radiation Laboratories. International collaboration on a high-temperature gas-cooled reactor (DRAGON) has involved, as previously noted, the United Kingdom, EURATOM, and other members of the OECD.

The more than one dozen research and experimental reactors operated by the authority account for the major portion of the total nuclear research effort. Through contractual arrangements, universities undertake certain basic research, but research by private industry has so far been confined mainly to areas which require little in the way of special facilities. In 1957, a National Institute for Research in Nuclear Science was set up to help provide certain expensive facilities and equipment for common use by universities and others who individually could not afford to purchase them. The governing board is made up of representatives from the UKAEA, the University Grants Committee, the Royal Society, and the Department of Scientific and Industrial Research. Funds are provided by means of Exchequer grants through the UKAEA.

The need for special training courses has been met, as in the United States, in part by employing the facilities within government research establishments and in part by relying on the universities. For basic scientific training, the universities and technical colleges are becoming increasingly well equipped and are even introducing new courses tailored to the new technology. But for short courses aimed at a broad range of users of radio-active materials and industrial operators, the authority's own establishments have served as the major training centers. The Reactor School at Harwell, the Isotope School at Wantage and the Operations School at Calder Hall are the three main contributors of courses for the technical staff of private firms, overseas students, university teachers, electricity industry staff, and so on. The practice of seconding staff from the universities and industry to work for longer periods in the authority's scientific establishments provides an important supplementary educational contribution.

Turning to the arrangements for the development of nuclear energy for civil, commercial applications, we find a complex interplay between the UKAEA, the nationalized electricity industry, and a number of private firms. This partnership between government and business was realized soon after the war in accordance with terms announced in the House of Commons on March 14, 1956.[10] The authority impinges on private industry in a variety of ways. It is a large buyer of plants, buildings and equipment for its own use, and, as such, it makes a substantial contribution to the business of the construction and engineering industries and a rather less significant contribution to that of a range of smaller trades. There are, in fact, few firms capable of undertaking the contracts for a big project; some twenty civil engineering firms bid for these jobs, and several thousand firms are on the authority's lists to supply all its needs.

Construction of the nuclear power stations is entrusted to private industry under contract to the Central Electricity Generating Board and the South of Scotland Electricity Board—not to the authority itself. These undertakings are so much beyond the resources of a single firm that the government encouraged several firms to come together to form consortia. There were originally five of these, but the number was reduced to four in 1960 following the announced policy of cutting back the nuclear-power program. The number of consortia was subsequently reduced to three by amalgamations. Each consortium consists basically of a firm of electrical engineers, a firm of constructional engineers, and a firm of boilermakers. Altogether about fifteen firms have been drawn together into the three consortia. There are various arrangements for pooling information, but the consortia compete, at least in form, for power-station contracts. There is also a collaborative program which provides the consortia with experimental facilities for the nuclear-physics aspects of reactor design.

The authority's position is akin to that of a broker standing between the nationalized electricity industry as purchaser and the members of the consortia as sellers. Representation of two possibly conflicting interests is made possible by employing different sections within the authority to advise the two respective parties to the contract. This arrangement is not entirely

[10] Central Office of Information, *op. cit.*, pp. 9–10.

satisfactory but has apparently been an unavoidable consequence of the limited number of expert personnel available. In
1963, liaison between the Atomic Energy Authority and the
Central Electricity Generating Board was improved by giving
the latter representation on an advisory committee that deals
with programs for the nuclear generation of power. Despite this
development, there has been mounting criticism of the apparent
division of responsibility between the two government agencies
most concerned. In June, 1963, this criticism reached a climax
when Lord Coleraine resigned from the numerous offices he held
in several of the firms of one consortium in order to launch an
aggressive campaign in the House of Lords against what he considered to be a general "muddle" in atomic-energy administration, more particularly against the growing autocracy of the
Central Electricity Generating Board. He contended:

> On the one hand, the United Kingdom Atomic Energy Author-
> ity is supported by millions of public money to develop nuclear
> energy, on the other hand the C.E.G.B., which has, so far as I
> know, no constitutional responsibility for nuclear energy, is the
> determining authority simply because it is the only customer for
> nuclear power stations in this country.[11]

In its relations with each consortium, the authority takes
the major share of responsibility for investigating and establishing the scientific and technical feasibility of the new reactor
systems up to and including the prototype stage. The consortium
then assumes the main responsibility for development modifications and commercial exploitation. The consortia are not wholly
excluded from the preliminary design and prototype stage, nor
is the authority precluded from tendering advice, where necessary, at the second stage. The continuing involvement of the
authority and private industry in all stages is an administrative
commentary on the generalization already made—namely, that
it is impossible to establish a clear cutoff point between research
and development, on the one hand, and commercial application,
on the other. The fact, too, that the nationalized electricity authority, the chief customer, has also seen fit in recent years to

---

[11] *The Times* (London), June 24, 1963, p. 10. The debate on Lord Coleraine's motion to set up a special committee of inquiry is reported in *The
Times,* July 11, 1963, p. 14.

devote an annual sum of £1,000,000 to research and development for nuclear power production provides additional confirmation of the complexities of these relationships.[12]

The groups now making up three consortia appear relatively stable, if not already closed to other firms. The existing firms are being associated with the development of reactors of an advanced type, chiefly by seconding staff to the authority, which seems to indicate that it is these firms who will be responsible for construction if prototypes prove commercially feasible. Nevertheless, other firms in joint association or, in some cases, in conjunction with firms from the United States are not precluded from bidding for tasks falling outside the construction of power-generating stations. Some are engaged on contract research into metallurgy and materials, others on reactors for propulsion of submarines or aircraft, and still others on cheaper methods of producing the heavy water used as a moderator. These and similar tasks associated with the industrial applications of nuclear energy have resulted in the formation of various conferences and committees designed to help industry co-ordinate these varied efforts: chief among these are the Nuclear Energy Trade Associations' Conference, the British Nuclear Energy Conference, and the Nuclear Energy Committee of the Council of the Institute of Metals.[13]

Certain criticisms of these collaborative arrangements between the authority and private industry have been voiced. The authority must follow the policy imposed on all public bodies by the government of using competitive tenders in placing its contracts—and, in fact, about sixty per cent of the authority's contracts are put out to tender. Since the preparation of a tender for a power station is estimated at about £250,000 for each consortium, it has been argued that it would be much less wasteful to place orders openly by rotation and have the electrical authorities, as the purchasers, check contractors' costs, profit margin, and performance. The problem of competitive bidding for the right to construct plants for the electricity board was forced to a head in June, 1963, when the board apparently changed its

---

[12] "The Broken Promise of Atomic Power" *Sunday Times* (London), Colour Magazine Section, December 2, 1962, pp. 14–19.

[13] Central Office of Information, *op. cit.*, pp. 35–36.

mind about using two consortia for the construction at Wylfa, Anglesey, of what will be the largest nuclear power plant in the world—1,000 MW. It was the board's decision to rely on one consortium that triggered the resignation of Lord Coleraine and the critical debate in the House of Lords.

Further criticism is directed at the high royalties charged by the authority for the information it provides to private firms. The justification for these charges is that the information has been acquired by the authority at public expense. On the other hand, British firms which are expected to fulfill export orders find themselves placed at a competitive disadvantage in winning these markets. In general, they think that too hard a bargain has been struck, considering the large element of risk which the uncertain future of nuclear-generated power holds for them and the substantial "national interest" components of their work. In pursuing this policy, of course, the authority is simply obeying the government's instructions to operate on strict "commercial" lines wherever it can. The collaborating private firms, as well as the nationalized electricity industry, are inclined to believe that they are being called upon to bear more than their fair share of the development costs involved in pioneering civil applications of nuclear energy.

The major problems on the developmental side of this program in Britain stem from the declared policy of using nuclear power to meet the expected shortage in power generated by more conventional means. In the definiteness and size of this commitment, the United Kingdom stands alone among the countries under review. This policy also marks a striking departure from the previously described situation in the United States. There the supply of energy from conventional sources will be supplemented only to a very small extent by any commercially feasible nuclear power plants; but, more important, such nuclear power as does become available will be distributed through the normal channels of public or private utilities. In the United Kingdom, however, it is expected that nuclear-generated power will, by 1968, constitute one-eighth of total power output and that all of it will be produced and distributed through the present nationalized system.

The difficulty of planning for future development and making the correct decisions, even in the short run, can be emphasized by taking brief note of the technical complications involved. Reactors built to produce plutonium or for experimental purposes all produce heat, and if this heat is transferred to steam generators, electricity can be produced in commercial quantities. It was this knowledge that led to the construction of the world's first industrial-scale power station at Calder Hall, the prototype for larger stations which are now being commissioned or are still under construction for the British electricity authorities. Just as the reactors built for other than power purposes are capable of producing power as a by-product, so those built for producing power on a commercial scale are capable of producing plutonium as a by-product. This by-product is, in turn, the fuel for the "fast-breeder" reactors on which current research is concentrated because the ultimate commercial feasibility of nuclear power would appear to depend on their successful development.

It is the reactor designed primarily for power production which has been and is being constructed by the consortia for delivery to the electricity authorities. Although based on the same reactor technology employed in the Calder Hall plant—fueled with natural uranium, moderated by graphite, and cooled by gas under pressure—this reactor's continuous improvements have increased original estimates of output and have lowered estimated costs.[14]

In planning the future of nuclear power programs, then, there are a number of complex variables to be taken into consideration, and changes in these have necessitated a series of revisions in long-range plans. Approximately a decade elapses between the first feasibility study and the commissioning of a power reactor. In that interval, £20,000,000 may be spent, divided equally between the research and developmental costs and the capital costs of construction. With nine commercial nuclear power plants already commissioned or under construction and a probable three projected for the future, it is clear that a continual process of adapting design and construction must take

---

[14] Detailed descriptions of the reactors in use or under construction can be found in *ibid.*, pp. 55–63.

place in order to incorporate the results derived from reactors already in operation. This variability inherent in the rapidly developing state of reactor technology is compounded by another set of variables: the atom itself is competing with conventional sources of energy, notably coal and oil in Britain, and the supply and costs of these sources must be taken into account in seeking to determine the relative competitive advantages of using each one. Nor is the technology relating to conventional sources at a standstill; the improved design of coal-fired stations makes possible a much enlarged productive capacity which, in turn, forces a fresh evaluation in the nuclear power field.

The policies announced in successive governmental white papers reflect the difficulties which these variables create for decision-makers. In 1955, the first pronouncement envisaged the completion of twelve nuclear power stations with a total output of 1,500–2,000 MW by the end of 1965. Two years later, as a result of design changes inspired by the performance of the Calder Hall station, together with a growing concern over the nation's total energy needs, the projected output was set at 5,000 to 6,000 MW. It was still assumed that nuclear power would compete on roughly equal terms with conventional power by 1965. By 1960, this initial optimism had been considerably dampened: advances in thermal technology, lowering of earlier estimates of the operating costs of conventional power stations, raising of estimates for nuclear power stations, and changes in the supply and prices of coal and oil all combined to bring about a major policy revision. The white paper issued in 1960 cut back the program by one-half: the 6,000 MW output was not to be attained until 1970, and, by 1966, the seven power stations then expected to be in full operation would produce only 3,000 MW. The critical point at which these stations are expected to compete economically with conventional power was also pushed back to 1970 or later.

The implications of the revisions, so far as the nationalized electricity industry is concerned, are painfully clear; it is being asked to buy at high cost a network of power stations whose economic operation is far from assured. It is small consolation to the industry to be assured that there is no other way of determining whether, in fact, nuclear power is an economic proposition, or that by encouraging design it will contribute to the establishment of a viable nuclear power system at some now rather indefinite date in the 1970's. The price of collaboration is indeed high, and, in the larger perspective of the national interest, it is too early either to count the cost or to judge whether the great nuclear gamble will pay off.

France. In France, research into the wide range of peaceful applications of nuclear energy is conducted primarily in establishments operated by the Atomic Energy Authority. Universities and, to a lesser extent, industries participate but always subject to state regulations designed to protect the health and safety of those who use radioactive materials and reactors. The equipment and resources required for research are, of course, extremely expensive, and, particularly in France, geographical and other factors have led to the concentration of such equipment in research centers and to correspondingly close working relations with the universities. In the United States and in Japan and Canada to a lesser extent, expensive facilities tend to be sited at universities where, particularly in basic research, there is less need to preserve such an intimate association with governmental scientific establishments.[15]

The first nuclear research establishment was set up by the Atomic Energy Authority at Fontenay-aux-Roses, the site of the first nuclear pile, ZOE. By 1948, the rapid acceleration of intramural research necessitated the creation of a second establishment at Saclay, now the largest nuclear research establishment in France. Subsequently, two more centers were created at Grenoble and Cadarache. Each has tended to concentrate on particular aspects of the research spectrum: Fontenay works especially on controlled fission, mineralogy, and health problems; Saclay, on fuels, moderators, and isotopes; Grenoble conducts research on the chemical, biological, and physical aspects of nuclear energy and operates particle accelerators; Cadarache investigates the nature of different types of atomic piles and the behavior of fuels and elements in reactors.

The urgent need to staff these establishments with properly

[15] "The University and Nuclear Education" in *Education and Nuclear Energy, op. cit.*

trained scientists, engineers, and technicians at a time when the country was rebuilding its war-torn resources forced a rapid improvisation of training courses conducted within the establishments themselves—particularly at Saclay. These courses were later opened to students from universities and engineering schools, a step which raised questions concerning the future role of the universities in the program. The somewhat unique method of resolving this issue was to have courses conducted jointly by teachers from the universities and from the research establishments. In 1956, this experiment culminated in the formation of a National Institute of Nuclear Science and Technology operated by a large representative board: twelve members from the Ministry of Education, twelve from the authority, and four from other interested ministries. The institute grants a one-year diploma to postgraduate nuclear engineers and a two-year diploma for graduates seeking further training in quantum mechanics, accelerator techniques, radiology, or nuclear power technology. All courses are conducted in collaboration with a number of universities.

Through the facilities provided at Saclay, many other educational and training programs are conducted directly by the staff. In addition, the Atomic Energy Authority offers bursaries and scholarships designed to attract students to the specialized courses given by laboratories associated with the universities and supported by the authority. Further assistance is provided by research contracts with the universities and the National Research Council.

For the developmental and commercial application of nuclear energy, France has tended to adopt much the same sort of collaborative approach with industry that has been such a striking feature of the programs in other countries. The Atomic Energy Authority has drawn heavily on the resources and skills of private engineering and construction firms. These, in turn, have had to create special divisions or even special subsidiaries to concentrate on the research and development of all aspects from raw materials to finished products. The complexity and costliness of these endeavors has also induced firms to group together, rather like the consortia in the United Kingdom, to pool their resources and particular technical skills and to share the costs. Thus, the Société des Potasses et Engrais Chimiques aided in the construction of a plant at Bouchet and, together with another group, the Compagnie Saint-Gobain, constructed the refinery at Malversi. For the design and construction of the important reactors at Marcoule, the authority brought together no less than four private groups. The Loire-Penhoet group engineered the work on the EL3 reactor at Saclay; the Indatom group has constructed other nuclear piles. The fabrication of special metals, electronic and mechanical equipment, and ceramics, as well as the production of moderators such as graphite and heavy water, has all been undertaken by private firms, often in collaboration with the Atomic Energy Authority or the French Electricity Authority, whose interest in nuclear-generated power is already quite extensive.

The actual production of nuclear-generated power is still very much a side line of reactors designed primarily for producing plutonium. The French Electricity Authority has assumed responsibility for the construction of generating plants designed to take off and employ some of the heat generated in the reactors, but as yet the electricity provided for the national grid constitutes only a token proportion of the total, and at present there are no plans, comparable to those in Britain, for example, to embark on an extended program of nuclear generating plants. Indeed, at the ministerial meetings of the Council for Europe in 1962 where the problems of a common market in energy were discussed, all attention was directed to the future of the conventional energy sources. It would appear that most of the world is inclined to move cautiously, pending the results of the experiments in Britain primarily, but also in the United States and, to a lesser extent in Canada, which is employing an entirely different technology.[16]

The collaboration between government and private firms in the developmental phases of nuclear energy has brought about the same formation of private organized interests as has occurred,

---

[16] However, it should be noted that EURATOM's five-year program (1963–1967) shows a doubling of its budget over the previous five years from $215,000,000 to $480,000,000, and some of these funds are directed to setting up power reactors in Italy and France.

for example, in the United Kingdom. One of these, the Association Technique pour la Production et l'Utilisation de l'Energie
Nucléaire, bands together more than two hundred members to
serve as a documentation center and promotional group. Another,
the Groupe Inter-Syndical de l'Industrie Nucléaire, is a trade association which represents the interests of nuclear industries in
France and cuts across the many professional organizations having a concern in the new technology.[17]

Canada. Although Canada, as a major producer of source
materials, has had especially complex problems to contend with,
these are dwarfed by the extensive range of activities and programs associated with the research and developmental aspects of
the nuclear-energy program. As a country with limited financial
and scientific resources, Canada in particular has felt the pressure of the vastly accelerated pace which has characterized developments in these fields. Reference has already been made to the
important consequences of the shortened period between the
prospecting stage and the delivery of refined materials; it has
brought on a major problem of overproduction probably unique
in Canada's mining history.[18] The same shortening of the time
sequence between basic and applied research has also typified
developments in this new sphere. The point was made by W. J.
Bennett, president of Atomic Energy of Canada Ltd., in 1956:

> Normally there is a time-lag between scientific discoveries and
> their practical application on any substantial scale. This means
> that the cost of research and the costs of applied work (design,
> engineering, development and fabrication) are usually spread over
> a considerable period. In the case of atomic energy, this time-lag
> has been reduced to the barest minimum. In fact, we have a some-

[17] For details, consult the useful booklet published by the Atomic Energy
Authority, *Commissariat à l'Énergie Atomique, 1945–1960* (1960), p. 63.
[18] Prof. F. A. Forward, director of the recently created Uranium Research
Foundation, has remarked: "Every metal has a life history which is a history
of growth. . . . In some metals this growth curve has lasted over five thousand years: for example, lead. Aluminum has come in the past one hundred
years. . . . Uranium has come in the past fifteen years; so you have a
completely new industry." See his evidence before Canada, House of Commons, Special Committee on Research, *Minutes of Proceedings and Evidence*
(Ottawa: Queen's Printer, 1956), p. 202.

what unique situation in that a large-scale research program and a large-scale applied program are being carried on simultaneously.[19]

A special Crown company, Atomic Energy of Canada Ltd., was set up to preside over the research and developmental program for the peaceful uses of atomic energy. Research was first undertaken as part of a wartime partnership in which Canadian scientists were assigned the task of working on a reactor which used natural uranium and was moderated with heavy water. The work was centered at Chalk River, until recently a government company town, which is situated 150 miles up the river from the nation's capital. In 1952 the project was segregated from the parent body, the National Research Council, and assigned specifically to the company. As in other countries, rapid growth of research necessitated the creation, in 1959, of a second major research installation at Whiteshell, Manitoba.

The oppressive costs of research, the great range of scientific, engineering, and technical skills (many of them, incidentally hitherto almost beyond the experience and training of Canadians) forced a near monopoly on Atomic Energy of Canada Ltd. Most research and nearly all the special training required have, for this reason, been conducted within the government's own facilities. The research and developmental facilities of private industry, upon which the government might otherwise have drawn, are in no way comparable to those available in the United States. Indeed, as one Canadian official has noted: "The parent companies of our Canadian fabricators [mainly firms in the United States] have decided to take all the economic risks they can afford in their home territory." [20] In short, the very success attained by the Atomic Energy Commission of the United States in enlisting the support of private firms has tended to constrict the amount of co-operation obtainable from their branch plants in Canada.[21]

[19] *Ibid.,* pp. 239–240.
[20] See the statement of J. L. Gray before sessions of the Canadian Nuclear Association, reported in *Globe and Mail* (Toronto), May 18, 1961.
[21] Just as American mining interests were able, in effect, to export their surplus problems to Canada, so, too, has the cost of research been exported to Canadian branch plants of American companies.

106 ADMINISTERING THE ATOM FOR PEACE

The financial support which the United States government has been willing to provide for research and development in private firms goes far beyond anything the Canadian government has been prepared to give. Even the National Research Council's announcement in 1961 that the support of industrial research would be extended by financing up to half the costs falls well below the generous standards in the United States where industry, on the average, contributes from its own financial resources roughly only ten per cent of its research expenditures.

Historically, the National Research Council has concentrated on building up a cadre of trained scientists by directing most of its grants to universities. The council's support of university graduate work in the sciences between the two world wars has provided a strong base for supplying the mounting need in the postwar period for the scientific skills without which the present ambitious nuclear-energy program could not have been launched at all. This support has been in the form of fellowships to individuals and grants for equipment and projects undertaken in university laboratories. This pattern has been repeated in nuclear research, the council serving as the selection agency for the Atomic Energy Control Board and assigning specific pieces of expensive equipment, such as cyclotrons and accelerators, to particular universities. On the other hand, the government's own research establishments, as in other countries, have served as training centers, offering short courses on particular aspects of nuclear energy in its basic and applied fields.

The same pattern of state domination is found in the developmental and commercial exploitation of the atom in Canada—for roughly the same reasons that leave the initiative for research in the hands of specialized governmental agencies. However, as has been true of other countries, a major effort has been made to enlist the help of private firms, especially for the development of nuclear-generated power.

The power program stems, as elsewhere, from the reactors built for experimental purposes. The first of these (Zero Energy Experimental Pile—ZEEP) went active in September, 1945, and is still functioning. Two years later, the National Research Experimental (NRX) reactor was commissioned, its originally projected output of 10,000 KW of heat subsequently being raised to 30,000 KW. This reactor broke down in 1952, and history was made when, instead of being scrapped, it was repaired and re-activated with greater heat potential than it had previously possessed. Design for a third reactor, the National Research Universal (NRU), with five times the power of NRX, was authorized in 1950, and in November, 1951, this reactor was also commissioned. It is interesting to note that this is the only Canadian reactor capable of producing plutonium as a by-product. Since reactor technology in Canada is based on natural uranium, and there is no military program, all plutonium is shipped to the United States.

For the erection of these installations, Atomic Energy of Canada Ltd. has assumed primary responsibility in providing the research and developmental data and has paid for the nuclear components of the plants. Private firms have provided both money and professional or technical staff for the design, development, and construction of the stations. This partnership was extended in 1961 by associating a large provincially owned electrical utility in the erection of an improved nuclear-power demonstration plant (NPD2). Located at Rolphton, a short distance from the original Chalk River site, the plant is capable of producing a modest 20,000 KW of electricity which is purchased by the Ontario Hydro Commission, the participating utility.

Even as this pilot plant was being designed and constructed, a more ambitious project was set afoot. In 1957, the Nuclear Power Group, composed of engineers who were drawn from the power industry and stationed at Chalk River as a branch of Atomic Energy of Canada Ltd., presented a report on a full-scale reactor fueled with natural uranium and moderated with heavy water. The government not only approved the decision to go forward but in July, 1959, before the design and development phase was completed, authorized the construction of the Canadian Deuterium Uranium (CANDU) plant in order to gain immediate experience with a large-scale installation. Ontario Hydro, possibly the only electrical utility sufficiently favorably placed to make economic use of nuclear-generated power, agreed to collaborate. Major components for the new plant are being ordered by competitive tender and fixed price bids, wherever possible from Canadian suppliers, who are gradually becoming educated to the demands of the atom age.

The site for CANDU was determined by Ontario Hydro in its capacity as the commercial user of the end product. Atomic Energy of Canada pays for the cost of the station, and Ontario Hydro will operate it and purchase the power at a rate which will be comparable with rates for equivalent power produced from conventional sources. This arrangement should eliminate the criticism directed at the British scheme, which tends to saddle the Central Electricity Generating Board with uneconomical power plants in this trial period. Ultimately, Atomic Energy of Canada will sell the plant to Ontario Hydro for a sum based on performance, cost of fuel, and other relevant factors. Commercial operation is scheduled for 1965.

In order to grapple effectively with this rapidly expanding portion of the program, Atomic Energy of Canada set up a Nuclear Power Plant Division. Reflecting the intimate collaboration with Ontario Hydro in this venture, the division is actually located at Toronto in headquarters provided by Hydro and partially staffed from that agency's own engineering division. Further additions to staff have been made by inducing other utilities, manufacturers, and firms of consulting engineers to lend personnel for training and experience. Indeed, the staff now mirrors not only the unusual partnership between scientific and professional persons in government and private firms, but also a genuine international collaboration which brings together experts from the United States, Britain, Sweden, and EURATOM.

Further evidence of this type of co-operation is provided by the contract made with Canadian General Electric by Atomic Energy of Canada to undertake preliminary designs for a new reactor using a coolant cheaper than heavy water. The basic research on the properties of the organic materials in the coolant is being conducted by the Chalk River chemical and metallurgical groups with the intention of using the new reactor as the core of the recently approved Nuclear Research Establishment at Whiteshell. Sponsorship by AECL of a private study of the possibility of using small "packaged" reactors, run on enriched fuel, in certain remote areas of the North is but another illustration of collaboration; the Canada-India Reactor commissioned at Trombey, India, is a notable extension of such collaborative arrangements on an international scale. The reactor, under the auspices of the Colombo Plan, has been designed and built by a combination of private contractors and engineers and government scientific staff. Indian scientists, engineers, and operators have been trained in Canada in preparation for taking over when Atomic Energy of Canada is satisfied with its operation. The reactor provides an opportunity for scientists and engineers throughout the Colombo Plan countries to gain experience in the new technology.

The increasing involvement of private industry in Canada's atomic-energy program has produced, as in other countries, various associations designed to encourage research or, more generally, to provide centers of information and public education. Chief among these are the Canadian Nuclear Association, which sponsors occasional conferences, and the Uranium Research Foundation, which is seeking in particular to find new uses for the metal.

Surveying the field which Atomic Energy of Canada has come to occupy, it is clear that government policy has not been deliberately designed to confer a state monopoly. It has not been easy to overcome the reluctance of private enterprise to pioneer new commercial country. This difficulty is an ancient one, despite the widely cherished myth that Canadians view their country as a youthful, free-enterprise community. History and economic facts have seldom supported the myth; most major developments in transportation, communication, and even exploitation of natural resources have been pioneered by foreign capital or by the government itself. In this context, then, the hesitancy with which private enterprise has approached the peaceful exploitation of atomic energy is neither unique nor unexpected.[22]

Experience indicates that the usual sequence of events follows a fairly consistent pattern: having entered a certain field, the government becomes too deeply committed, in terms of capital

---

[22] This generalization could be applied, for example, to Canadian experience over the past generation with air transport and broadcasting.

investment and large establishments, to retreat once the risky pioneering stage is over; at this turning point, private enterprise usually begins to recognize the opportunities for profit which governmental initiatives have made possible, and pressure builds up to induce the government to abandon its enforced monopoly position.

In the case of atomic energy, it would appear that the process of delineating the appropriate roles of the public and private sectors may well evolve at the same rapid pace as has the technological development of nuclear energy. Key government officials have been striving to obtain a committed collaboration from the private sector. Possessing no powers other than those of persuasion, backed by substantial public funds, they have alternately praised and scolded private enterprise.[23] The official conception of the respective roles of government and private industry appears to be that the main responsibility for research should rest on governmental shoulders but, to a much greater extent than current practice seems to promise, the private sector should assume major responsibility for development, engineering, manufacturing, and, ultimately, operations.

Japan. From the beginnings of industrialization in the late nineteenth century in Japan, industry has relied on imported technology. Technical license fees paid to foreign firms have constituted an important part of the cost of research and development. The declared policy of achieving technological and scientific self-sufficiency in atomic energy, therefore, signalizes a distinct departure from this tradition and has placed the government at the forefront of the research and developmental program.

The Japan Atomic Energy Research Institute is the chief instrumentality of the state in implementing the program; nearly sixty per cent of the total atomic-energy budget is invested in

---

[23] Members of Parliament went out of their way, at successive sessions of the Special Committee on Research, to charge representatives of the private sector with their unenterprising qualities—a view frequently echoed by W. J. Bennett when he was president of Atomic Energy of Canada. (See, for example, his paper "Canadian Industry and Atomic Energy," which appears as an appendix to *Minutes and Proceedings and Evidence,* Special Committee on Research, *op. cit.*)

the work of this agency. Additional research is conducted in the government's National Institute of Radiological Sciences and, to a lesser extent, in the Atomic Fuel Corporation. Like the government research establishments set up in other countries, the Atomic Energy Institute has been compelled to assume a dominant role in providing the instruction for its own staff as well as for the university and industrial personnel who are working on specific aspects of the program. The concern to preserve the traditional independence of the universities has been particularly pronounced in Japan. When the Diet approved the act setting up the Atomic Energy Commission, it specifically requested that the expenditures for research in universities be excluded from review by the commission. Although the atomic-energy budget, for this reason, does not include expenditures on university research, the Long Range Program distinctly includes the expected contribution from universities in its plans. In fact, three nuclear reactors have been installed in universities, two more are in private firms, and the remainder is concentrated in the facilities of the Atomic Energy Research Institute. Universities contribute to policy formation by being fully represented on a number of specialist committees that advise the Atomic Energy Commission, while the views of the Japan Science Council have provided an objective and sometimes critical counterweight to other organizations concerned with the research and developmental aspects of the program.

Industry has also been drawn into research and development in a variety of ways. A nominal share of the capital invested in the research institute is contributed by private industry. However, the very presence of the institute, dedicated as it is to developing technological self-sufficiency in the field of nuclear energy, tends to place it in opposition to the traditional interests of private industry, which have been geared to importing the required technology through licensing agreements. As a direct offset to the state's unusual intervention, all the firms and organizations involved in nuclear-energy development have joined the Japan Atomic Industrial Forum. Set up in 1956, the forum has tended to decry the expenditure of public funds for research and development, favoring instead the traditional modes of importing the technology required. Nevertheless, the determination of the government to hold the initiative is clearly reflected in the fact that nearly one-third of the government's total expenditures for the development of science and technology is invested in atomic energy and less than five per cent of this portion is used to support private industrial research.

This latent conflict between the government and private firms is reflected in the arrangements devised for exploiting the power potential of the atom. The electric industry in Japan is composed of nine private companies and one mixed enterprise, the Power Resources Development Company. When the first full-scale power reactor was introduced from the United Kingdom, competition broke out between these two sets of interests for control of the reactor. As a means of placating both sides, a new body was created. The Japan Atomic Power Development Company was set up to include the interests of both private and public power companies, together with a contribution from the electrical-machine industry. This company is now building the first nuclear power plant. Although the reluctance of private concerns to accept a system of government subsidization was respected, the mixed method of financing still leaves the government in a commanding position.

No such antipathy to governmental help has been expressed by the shipbuilding industry in approaching its task of developing nuclear-propelled ships. It is therefore likely that, as this part of the nuclear-energy program builds up, there will be a much closer and more willing collaboration between government and the relevant private interests.

Italy. The organization for handling the research and developmental aspects of a peacetime nuclear-energy program in Italy is still at the formative stages. The earliest efforts to embark on research were, in fact, initiated by a semi-private group, the Studies and Experience Information Center of Milan. Direct government involvement did not occur until 1953 when the National Committee for Nuclear Research and the National Physics Institute were set up. Despite the improved status conferred on the committee by the shortened bill of 1960, it is still very

much in the position of an advisory body to the relevant departments, particularly the Ministry of Industry and Commerce,
which has operating responsibilities for nuclear-energy matters.
In addition to exercising certain inspecting and technical control
functions, the committee administers grants to universities for
nuclear research.

Basically, the difficulties and delays encountered by the various attempts to formulate a nuclear-energy law and to create a
strong state mechanism comparable to that of other countries
may be attributed to uncertainty over the respective roles of the
state and private enterprise in developing nuclear power.[24] Until very recently the electrical-power industry has been in private hands, and, since the earliest initiatives on research and
development were in fact promoted by private firms, there is
a strong body of opinion which holds that there is no need to
nationalize nuclear power. The fact that large capital resources
beyond the reach of private enterprise will be needed to exploit
nuclear power suggests, on the other hand, the need for considerable state support, if not outright ownership. Moreover, long-
range plans to industrialize southern Italy depend on the availability of power, which may best be provided by nuclear generators. The financial risks, as well as the technical hazards to health
and safety arising from such nuclear-power programs, add further
weight to the argument for a direct and heavy involvement of
the state. Further, the conditions imposed by EURATOM when
any one of its participating members, like Italy, launches a collaborative nuclear-reactor project entail strict state supervision.

The outlines of a likely course of collaborative action, similar
to that which has emerged in other countries, appear in the second part of the 1960 bill. The bill envisages a system of concessions administered by the Ministry of Industry and Commerce,
whereby private firms will be permitted to build nuclear power
plants, while the plants used for the production of special fissile

---

[24] The complexities of intermeshing governmental and private bodies in
economic affairs is well developed in Chapman, *op. cit.,* pp. 57–61. "Such is
the extent of the Italian State's share in the national economy that if its
true powers were exercised Italy could be transformed overnight, without
further legislation, into the most advanced socialist society in western Europe."

materials will be reserved for state-owned companies. The concessions would supplant the present system of authorizations which are issued to private firms after the features of the proposed plants have been scrutinized by the National Committee for Nuclear Energy. These authorizations provide a technical control over the siting and plans for the plant; there is no procedure for following up on the construction and operation of the plants, and none of them are to come into production, in any event, until 1963.[25] Since there are no plants for manufacturing uranium rods to fuel the reactors, the Ministry of Industry and Commerce also has the duty of controlling the trade in and safe use of these materials.

The proposed system of concessions leaves the state in a flexible position to grant or withhold rights in accordance with a planned program which recognizes the large element of public interest implicit in any nuclear power development. If the concessions are granted, the state can lay down strict provisions to safeguard the siting and use of the plant; it can ensure that the proper financial guarantees are provided and that construction will take place with specified cost and time limits. The implementation of such a concession system should permit the state to assume the initiative in the earlier stages of nuclear-energy development, when the commercial future of power plants is far from assured. As the program confirms its economic feasibility, more and more concessions can be awarded private firms, but always with the reservation to the state of the overriding responsibility for protecting the public interest.

International Research and Development. Just as the scarcity of scientific personnel and the high cost of conducting research and development in the field of atomic energy led various nations to concentrate their domestic resources in one or more state agencies, so have these factors fostered the proliferation of international or regional bodies dedicated to the same objectives.

[25] The legislation of December 6, 1962, which nationalized the electricity industry has now resolved this problem: the newly created National Board for Electric Energy will be responsible for operating all nuclear generating plants. The board is responsible to the minister of industry and commerce, who is also responsible for the National Committee for Nuclear Energy.

Joint efforts to train personnel, pool expensive equipment, exchange information, and assist in the application of specific aspects of nuclear technology have characterized this development.

The resolution passed in 1946 by the Assembly of the United Nations called for the establishment of a Commission on Atomic Energy under terms which included the "international exchange of basic scientific information for peaceful ends." This commission reported favorably on a proposal to set up an International Atomic Development Authority which, if the plans had been approved, would have placed in its hands all the intrinsically dangerous aspects of research and development, leaving national and private bodies to conduct peaceful operations.

The plans for this Development Authority were stillborn, but in the early 1950's, a number of regional co-operative enterprises came into being to construct such expensive equipment as particle accelerators for the study of high energy physics. These efforts were followed by a number of conventions concerned largely with establishing regulations to cover the use of nuclear materials, radiation hazards, and the like. In the late 1950's, experimental reactors were jointly established and operated on the initiative of the European Nuclear Energy Agency, the International Atomic Energy Agency, and EURATOM.

These bodies have significant programs for the collection and exchange of information developed in their member states. UNESCO has collaborated with such agencies and with individual nations in fostering world-wide conferences for broadening the range of scientific information on nuclear-energy developments. The training of scientists through national exchanges and scholarships has also been an important aspect of the internationalizing trend. An active collaborator in many of these efforts has been a non-governmental organization, the European Atomic Energy Society, made up of the atomic energy agencies of twelve Western European countries. This body is financed from both official and private sources, and its chief activity is arranging for meetings of scientists and engineers in different fields of applied nuclear research.

On the developmental side, similar collaboration on a regional or international basis has been achieved. EUROCHEMIC, a joint undertaking of the members of the Nuclear Energy Association (an adjunct to OECD), represents a combined effort to build and operate a plant and laboratory for processing irradiated fuels from reactors used for peaceful purposes and owned by the member states. The International Atomic Energy Agency acts as a clearing house for member states wishing to procure materials, equipment, or technical advice for building nuclear reactors. If financial support is also needed, the member states apply to the Technical Assistance Board of the United Nations and seek United Nations funds available either in the Expanded Program of Technical Assistance Fund or the Special Fund. The agreements between the International Agency and the applicant member assign to the agency a continuing supervisory role over the assisted activity. The contract programs financed by IAEA parallel those existing in each country between the atomic energy agency and the universities or industry. The research may provide the IAEA with information necessary to formulate an adequate regulatory program—for example, the study of biological effects of radiation as a preliminary to setting up health and safety standards; it may be to assist a laboratory or a scientist in a member state; or it may be to develop certain techniques, such as the use of isotopes for agricultural or medical research, that might be useful to member states. The only difference is that the International Agency is required to clear such matters at the official level by keeping the government of the member state fully informed of these agreements.

Even this sparse account of the general features of research and development at the supranational level is enough to reveal the extent and novelty of the arrangements which have all come into being over the past decade or so in response solely to the singular needs of this new source of energy. The old axiom that science knows no national boundaries could scarcely receive more convincing support than that found in this complex of relationships which has emerged almost overnight in the field of nuclear research and development.

VI
Regulation

Regulatory activities of the state now constitute a substantial portion of the day-to-day administrative burden falling on government in all countries. The police power is used to protect the lives and property of citizens; taxing and spending power, coupled with the control over money supply, is used to regulate the economy, redistribute incomes, and direct the flow of private and public investment; the safety and security of citizens traveling by land, sea, and air depend on state regulations; health is safeguarded by a host of licensing, inspecting, and other regulatory devices aimed at ensuring the purity of food and drugs, plants and animals; the citizen's pocketbook is guarded by regulations aimed at unfair advertising, unethical stock promotion, usurious rates of interest, discriminatory transportation rates, bank failures, and the like. In short, it is difficult to find any important area of community life or even individual practice that does not bear the imprint of the paternal regulatory hand of the state.

In this respect, nuclear energy is no exception. But there are certain features of the substances used, the processes involved, and the end products themselves which have demanded more thorough and comprehensive regulations than has been customary in most other fields of endeavor. Atomic energy is unique in requiring maximum regulation of every aspect, from the mining of the ore to the commissioning and subsequent operation of a nuclear plant. This is so partly because of the dual uses to which these materials, processes, and products may be put—they have both peaceful and warlike applications. The fabricated uranium metal may, for example, be used to fuel either a nuclear reactor geared to produce plutonium which is destined for military use or to a reactor destined to produce power. The same reactor may be simultaneously contributing to both peaceful and military purposes. This duality of purpose, particularly in the absence of universal agreement to control the military applications of atomic energy, enforces on each state the obligation to preserve a tight control over the supply of and trading in these substances, as well as a duty to regulate the processing stages and the disposition of the final products.

The second feature of atomic energy which gives rise to a special need for regulation is the intrinsic radioactive quality of the substances involved. Again, this calls for regulation of the uses to which the substances may be put, as well as ensuring that all necessary precautions are taken to safeguard the health of those who may be exposed to radiation hazards in the course of their research or in connection with processing and production. The problems of waste disposal, though not unique with nuclear-energy plants, are by all odds the most serious and likely to become more important as domestic applications are extended. Third, the regulations designed to safeguard the worker and community at large in carrying out industrial operations within a conventional plant must be particularly extensive and rigorously drawn when it comes to the siting, construction, and operation of a nuclear establishment, whether it be for research or industrial purposes.

Finally, the war-engendered atmosphere of secrecy, which has admittedly abated somewhat in the postwar period, still throws a mantle of regulations over the scientific "trade secrets" of each nation. The consequent stifling of the free flow of scientific information is an unhappy fact of life with which we must live as long as individual states hesitate to shackle the war-making potential of nuclear energy through international regulatory action.

Two factors have helped to perpetuate the seemingly unique features of atomic energy. First, the devastation wrought by the earliest and most primitive bombs is now known to be only a modest portent of the universal holocaust that newer bombs are capable of unleashing on the world. Consequently, there has been little reason for public opinion to discount, with the passing of time, the original fear and awe in which these nuclear weapons were held. Rather than breeding contempt, familiarity has given rise to a mounting fear and horror. It is within this mental climate that peacetime experimentation and development have had to proceed; since it is impossible to divorce the substances and processes required for peaceful applications from those used for military purposes, public opinion generally has supported the most rigorous regulation. Perhaps unduly aggravated by this fear, public anxiety has been alleviated only by imposing a regimen of controls which errs on the side of strictness. Certainly these regulations have contributed to inflating the already astronomical costs of conducting research and development in the peaceful uses of atomic energy.

Added to the natural public anxiety which must somehow be allayed by strict regulation, there is widespread ignorance on the part of a public, untutored in the intricacies of the new nuclear science and technology, concerning the nature and extent of the regulations really required. What is desirable and adequate by way of regulation is an issue on which a wide range of informed as well as lay opinion is held. In the circumstances, governments have leaned over backward to assure their peoples that every conceivable precaution has been taken. Time and increasing familiarity with the use of the new source of energy should, undoubtedly, produce some relaxation in the rigors of present regulations. But there will always be that residuum of almost unwholesome respect for the destructive power of the atom, and this will perpetuate the need for more than usually strict regulation, particularly as long as efforts to achieve international control continue to be frustrated.

It is within these parameters—both psychological and physical—that each state and the international community of states must approach the problems of regulating the peacetime uses of atomic energy. At least five important questions arise in connection with regulatory activities in this field.

    1. Who should promulgate the regulations?

    2. Who should administer them?

3. Given the large element of direct state involvement in the program, is it feasible and proper to employ the same state agency for regulatory as well as operating functions?

4. To what extent should the state itself become involved in direct operation of various elements of the program in order to fulfill its regulatory responsibilities?

5. On the supranational level, how far is it possible to develop international regulation of the peaceful uses of atomic energy as a substitute for or a supplement to national regulation?

The relevance of the experience of each of the countries surveyed in providing satisfactory answers to these questions constitutes the main burden of analysis in this chapter.

The United States. To the extent that government manages to divest itself of direct operating responsibilities in the field of research and development, the problems of regulation become more complex. The United States Atomic Energy Commission has been able to go further than its counterparts in other countries in making use of private industries and the universities to help implement the atomic-energy program. But although this arrangement reduces the direct operating responsibilities of the commission, it correspondingly increases the regulatory responsibilities. Widespread dispersion of nuclear and radioactive materials and the proliferation of research and industrial establishments using these materials in potentially hazardous reactors create major tasks of preserving adequate control over supply and distribution, the use and users of the materials and equipment. These tasks have, in the main, been assigned to the Atomic Energy Commission, although other agencies have been called upon to assume regulatory responsibilities in specific areas and will, no doubt, take over more as part of their normal regulatory activities.

The strictness of the regulations imposed on the production of nuclear materials varies with the nature of the materials. As previously indicated, source materials are not as closely controlled as special nuclear materials. Control over source materials is maintained by the contract purchasing procedures of the commission and by a system of commission licenses to authorize transfers, exports, or imports of such materials. The special nuclear materials such as plutonium and enriched uranium are subjected to much more rigorous controls. The president annually determines the quantity of such materials to be produced, and all of it is purchased or owned by the government. Private owners and operators of nuclear reactors pay the commission for the materials assigned to them under license, and licenses also cover any transfers between such operators. All trading in fissionable substances is equally subject to tight regulation: sales abroad can take place only where bilateral or multilateral agreements (of which there are now some forty in being) have been signed. AEC authorization is required, and the proceeds go to the government. Burned out fuel elements with unspent U_{235} or plutonium by-product are normally returned to the Atomic Energy Commission for reprocessing, and any fissionable material is purchased by the government. The production and use of radioactive isotopes, characterized as by-product material, is currently subject to AEC authorization but devolution to state regulatory agencies is in prospect. All high-level radioactive wastes are stored at government-owned sites located near the commission's reprocessing plants. Under AEC license, private persons can store low- and intermediate-level wastes prior to transportation (again under license) to the AEC permanent disposal grounds.

The assurance of the sound construction and safe operation of nuclear reactors is also part of the commission's regulatory assignment. It is responsible for the reactor safety program in connection with commission-owned reactors, and all other reactors —apart from those under the jurisdiction of the Defense Department—must be licensed. Licenses are granted only after a careful hearing and the receipt of a report on hazards prepared after an evaluation by AEC staff and the Advisory Committee on Reactor Safeguards. The commission must also grant the necessary construction permits and issue operating licenses.

It is not surprising to find that an agency organized on the basis of a single source of energy should duplicate, in its regulatory activities, many of the functions performed by other departments which have traditionally been responsible for the general health and safety of the nation. Thus, the Public Health Service of the Department of Health, Education, and Welfare, among other responsibilities, is expected to control water pollution; the Food and Drug Administration in the same department is responsible for evaluating the safety of foods, drugs, cosmetics, and therapeutic devices and for taking appropriate legal action to protect the public; the Department of Agriculture checks radiation in the agricultural environment and regulates the wholesomeness of meat and poultry. Similarly, the National Bureau of Standards in the Department of Commerce has a broad statutory charter to investigate radiation uses and hazards and to co-operate with government and private organizations in establishing standards. Safety in factories or in mines comes within the respective ambits of the Department of Labor and the Department of the Interior. Even the various agencies concerned with transportation and the mail—the Coast Guard, the Interstate Commerce Commission, the Federal Aviation Agency, and the Post Office— have responsibilities for regulating interstate commerce and foreign transport of radioactive substances.

In short, the Atomic Energy Commission is surrounded by agencies with long-established claims to jurisdiction over at least some elements of the regulatory process as applied to nuclear energy. Moreover, as an additional complication, regulation of health and safety has traditionally been shared between agencies of the national government and the agencies of the state or local governments. In fact, regulation of health hazards and radiation sources has normally evolved at the local level in response to local circumstances. The individual states entered the field to ensure uniformity, and the further need to achieve interstate uniformity brought the federal authorities into the picture. In the case of atomic energy, this evolutionary development has been reversed, for the Atomic Energy Commission at the outset assumed regulatory charge of the whole field, and it was not until 1959 that the Atomic Energy Act was amended to make provision for state regulation. Even so, the amendment continued to confer exclusive regulatory responsibility on the AEC for such matters as the construction and operation of reactors, the chemical processing of nuclear fuels, exports and imports of all types, and the disposal of wastes and materials. The amendment therefore applies principally to regulating the use of radioisotopes, and, since each state has long been responsible for control of radiation from other sources, their prospective assumption of AEC powers over radioactive isotopes should not constitute a very large additional burden. To date, however, the necessary AEC agreements with the governors of the respective states still await the assurance that state control programs are satisfactory.[1]

Despite present difficulties in reaching agreement with the states, it is clear that duplication of regulatory machinery for radiation control ought to be eliminated, for there seems to be little sense in an arrangement which confers powers on the federal government when the source of the radioactive material is a nuclear reactor and on the state government when the source is, for instance, a cyclotron. The other practical consideration that may delay the assumption by the states of this regulatory power is that industries using such radioactive materials operate in a number of states and would, therefore, have to deal with a multiplicity of state regulatory agencies rather than, as at present, with the Atomic Energy Commission alone.[2]

The extent to which the jurisdiction of other regulatory agencies, both federal and state, might overlap or conflict with AEC responsibilities was probably not fully recognized at the time the commission was established. The effort to avoid federal-state duplication made in the 1959 amendment to the Act has been extended to designing working arrangements between the AEC and other federal agencies that would minimize duplication of effort at the national level. Most effort has been directed to ironing out difficulties in the health and safety areas. The radiation program of the Department of Health, Education, and Welfare has been expanding rapidly; it constitutes the most important

---

[1] For existing state legislation in this field see the summary in Kruse, *op. cit.*, pp. 59–61.

[2] An excellent survey of federal-state relations in this regulatory area is to be found in Assembly of the State of California, Assembly Interim Committee on Public Health, Subcommittee on Radiation Protection, *Radiation Protection in California* (Sacramento, Calif.: 1961), Vol. IX.

area of potential conflict and has given rise to new machinery for co-ordination.

Prior to 1959, there was no official centralized arrangement in the executive branch for the formulation of radiation protection standards or guidance on their use. Each of the agencies mentioned with responsibilities in this field was free to formulate whatever standards it deemed appropriate within the bounds of its statutory powers. Growing public concern with respect to radioactive fallout and Congressional proposals to turn the Atomic Energy Commission's health and safety responsibilities over to the Public Health Service led the president, in 1959, to initiate a full review of the federal organization of radiation protection activities.

The review, conducted by the commission, the Department of Health, Education, and Welfare, and the Bureau of the Budget, recognized that successful peacetime radiation protection rested primarily on the development and formulation of standards. Such standards (which pertain to the radiation exposure individuals may receive and which serve as the basis for detailed operational standards) represent a balance between biological risks, on the one hand, and, on the other, the benefits to be gained from taking certain risks. Clearly, these decisions go beyond a purely scientific judgment, essential as the scientists' expert opinions are in assessing these risks. Accordingly, it was concluded that radiation protection standards and guidance involved a consideration of health, economic, social, and even ethical factors and that the person or persons making the ultimate decisions based on these multiple considerations should be publicly accountable.

The single agency which, up to 1959, had served as the primary source for recommendations on basic standards was the National Committee on Radiation Protection and Measurement. Since this committee was a non-governmental body composed of scientists drawn from government and private concerns, it lacked the element of accountability deemed desirable. And, since none of the existing agencies had either the necessary breadth of responsibility or fully represented all the relevant interests, it was necessary to devise a new procedure. In effect, the proposal was to vest the responsibility for promulgating the basic standards in the president himself. On August 14, 1959, the president accepted this recommendation, and, at the same time, established by executive order (later confirmed by statute) the Federal Radiation Council, an advisory body to assist him in performing this task. The council is essentially an interdepartmental committee representing the agencies most directly concerned with radiation protection—the Atomic Energy Commission and the departments of Health, Education, and Welfare; Commerce; Defense; and Labor, with the president's science advisor having the right to participate in council decisions. Technical advice is provided to the council by the relevant federal agencies, the National Committee on Radiation Protection and Measurements, the National Academy of Sciences, and other recognized authorities.

This new approach to the protection problems associated with the widespread application of nuclear energy is still relatively untried. That it is not without its own problems is clear from criticisms already directed against the council.[3] But a national organ of this type, buttressed by the prestige of the president, is clearly necessary if orderly and responsible regulation of radiation hazards is to be ensured.

The excessive caution which has characterized the regulatory operations of the Atomic Energy Commission has been accentuated by the law courts. The increasing number of civilian reactors, particularly those to be used for large-scale power-generation, has resulted in an intensification of public concern over the hazards factor. In turn, this concern has fostered the growth within the commission's regulatory divisions of what some critics consider to be an excessive reliance on judicial hearings.

The most controversial and significant of these legal actions has been the case of the fast-breeder power reactor under construction at Lagoona Beach, Michigan, on the shores of Lake Erie; the site is within a few miles of the urban centers of Detroit and Toledo. Controversy has centered on the alleged inadequacy of the procedures adopted for ensuring safe construction of the plant. At a minimum, it was held that the AEC should

[3] Joint Committee on Atomic Energy, *Radiation Protection Criteria and Standards: Their Basis and Use—Summary Analysis of Hearings* (Washington, D.C.: Government Printing Office, 1960).

impose the same safety requirements when it issues a construction permit as it does when it later issues an operating license and that designs should be completed and evaluated before construction is started. This contention was supported on the grounds that the safety determination should be made prior to construction; otherwise, it would be extremely difficult for the AEC to with-hold the operating license after millions of dollars of construction had been erected. The commission took the position that a requirement of this nature was unreasonable in view of the current state of reactor technology and that its acceptance might seriously impede or even block the development of atomic-power projects. The Court of Appeals ruled against the commission but, on appeal to the Supreme Court, on a majority decision, the issue was resolved in favor of the commission's stand.[4] The decision in this case was regarded as vitally significant to the commission's future exercise of its regulatory responsibilities. It was not only the first contested licensing procedure but, had the decision ultimately gone against the commission's views, would have added to the time-consuming, repetitive, and judicialized hearings against which there had already been much complaint.[5]

The Lagoona Beach case served to focus attention on one of the unique features of the Atomic Energy Commission: its combination of operational and regulatory responsibilities. There has been some fear expressed that the two functions are incompatible and should, therefore, be undertaken by two separate agencies. Obviously, regulatory problems assume increasing importance as the peaceful uses of atomic energy expand and as more and more interests become involved. The magnitude of these regulatory obligations has, in fact, encouraged a trend toward separating the two types of activities but keeping them under the same administrative roof. At the same time, as noted, there has been a substantial "judicialization" of the regulatory aspects of the commission's work.

[4] See *Power Reactor Development Co.* v. *International Union of Electrical, Radio and Machine Workers, AFL-CIO et al.,* Supreme Court of the United States, October term, 1960, decision of June 12, 1961. In the course of arguing the decision, Associate Justice William J. Brennan, Jr., for the court gave an excellent summary of the regulatory process.
[5] Staff of the Joint Committee on Atomic Energy, *Improving the AEC . . . , op. cit.,* p. 31.

The first move to effect this separation within the Atomic Energy Commission occurred in 1957 when the Division of Civilian Application, which was responsible for both regulation and promotion, was abolished and its functions transferred to two separate units: the Division of Licensing and Regulations and the Office of Industrial Development. Two years later, the increased emphasis on regulatory activities was signalized by the creation of a new position—the assistant general manager for regulations and safety. A further modification was made in March, 1961, when a new position, director of regulations, was established. It was indicative of the efforts to effect a clearer separation of the semi-judicial regulatory functions from the operative functions that the new director was authorized to report directly to the five-man commission rather than to the general manager. Hitherto, all divisions reported through the normal channels to the general manager who, as chief executive officer, was responsible to the commission for the day-to-day administration of all AEC responsibilities.[6]

These internal organizational changes, while stressing the need to effect a sharper separation of regulatory and operative functions, also confirm the original decision to leave both functions in the same agency. Since responsibility for regulation and operation is still combined at the level of the commission members, critics of present arrangements have not really been placated. The argument for a more complete separation rests on the need to ensure that objective consideration of vital safety factors will not be undermined by the zealous promotional program undertaken by the operating divisions within the same agency. Although this is a logical and legitimate concern, it may be that, at this juncture, more problems would be raised than would be solved by seeking a purist solution.[7] The current state of reactor tech-

---

[6] The hearing examiner, the secretary to the commission, and the general counsel were exceptional in having a direct reporting connection with the commission.

[7] The consensus of views taken by the Joint Committee on Atomic Energy in 1961 generally opposed a separate regulatory body divorced from the AEC, but there were many interesting suggestions for improving the procedures themselves; see Staff of the Joint Committee on Atomic Energy, *op. cit.*

nology is relatively unsettled; each reactor is, in a sense, unique, and each has its own special technical problems. Those charged with regulation must, therefore, have ready access to the most up-to-date technical information, and, at the moment, the chief repositories are the operating units of the commission, along with the Advisory Committee on Reactor Safeguards. Such ready access and close contact are obviously best obtained by housing the two activities under one roof.

It should also be observed that the alleged incompatibility between operations and promotion, on the one hand, and regulation, on the other, may be unduly exaggerated. In the long run, failure to ensure safe application of nuclear energy constitutes the greatest threat to promotion of its widespread use; misuse can only lead to more rigorous regulation. An agency simultaneously concerned with both regulation and promotion is perhaps the most likely to be impressed with the need to preserve a proper balance. Indeed, the excellent over-all safety record in the commission's own establishments and its responsible, conservative approach to regulation—reinforced, as noted, by the courts—seems to argue for the practical viability of the present combination of functions.

In a recent amendment to the Atomic Energy Act, dated August 29, 1962, two new provisions have been added which are obviously a legislative response to some of the criticisms of present regulatory practices. The first authorizes the commission to establish one or more

> . . . atomic safety and licensing boards, each composed of three members, two of whom shall be technically qualified and one of whom shall be qualified in the conduct of administrative proceedings, to conduct such hearings as the Commission may direct and make such intermediate or final decisions as the Commission may authorize with respect to the granting, suspending, revoking or amending of any license or authorization under the provisions of this Act, any other provision of law, or any regulation of the Commission issued thereunder.[8]

The intention of this new hearing machinery is to eliminate the criticism that the hearing examiner of the commission lacked

---

[8] Pub. L. 87–615, 87th Cong., S. 3491, August 29, 1962.

sufficient technical knowledge to render an acceptable decision on these complex licensing cases.

The other provision retains the public hearing on licensing cases but also provides that, in the absence of a request from interested parties, no further hearings need be held once the operating license has been granted. This section is an obvious follow-up on the Lagoona Beach decision and is directed toward the elimination of excessive or repetitive public hearings.

Finally, it should be recalled that, in performing its regulatory responsibilities, the Atomic Energy Commission is by no means alone or unchecked. It would appear that for nuclear energy, as is true throughout the system of American government, the tradition of checks and balances and the distrust of conferring a monopoly of power on one agency have not been without influence. The formulation of general regulations, as noted, is vested in the president. He himself is advised by a widely representative council which in turn can draw on a wealth of expert advice from within and from outside the government. In enforcing regulations through its licensing and inspecting powers, the commission has taken care to effect the internal organizational separation already described and has developed elaborate procedural safeguards. To these must be added the contributions made to the regulatory process by many other federal agencies, as well as the expected increasing intervention of state agencies.

The United Kingdom. The United Kingdom Atomic Energy Authority is, like its counterpart in the United States, vested with both operating and regulatory responsibilities. In marked parallel with American developments, and for much the same reasons, the UKAEA has reorganized its internal administrative units so as to achieve a practical separation between the operating groups and the Health and Safety Branch. The accident to the reactor at Windscale in 1957 precipitated this separation in response to the widespread public anxiety over radiation hazards. The branch tenders its advice directly to the governing board of the authority, in much the same fashion as the equivalent Division of Licensing and Regulation reports directly to the five-man Atomic Energy Commission in the United States. Board decisions are disseminated through the branch to the heads of the groups who are responsible for the safety of all operations under their respective commands. An internal inspectorate is provided by the branch to assess the safety of reactors and plants, and radiation standards, embracing employees and the public generally, are also formulated by the branch. It will be observed that, unlike the American situation, regulation in Britain is much more self-regulation in that so many more of the operations associated with the program are in government hands.

Another parallel with the situation in the United States is to be found in the sharing of regulatory powers between the authority and various other bodies whose normal lines of jurisdiction cut across nuclear energy. Indeed, it would appear that the traditional departments have tended to apply their general regulatory powers to nuclear energy much more extensively than has been the case in the United States. For example, disposal of radioactive wastes is not under the authority but is subject to authorization from the appropriate ministry—the Ministry of Housing and Local Government, the Ministry of Agriculture, Fisheries, and Food, and so on. These ministries are involved because of their respective responsibilities for environmental health matters, which include discharge of radioactive waste to air, water, or ground and radioactive contamination of water supplies, food, sewers, rivers, and so on. Similarly, the Home Office and the Ministry of Transport deal with questions arising from the transport of radioactive materials; medical use of radioisotopes and apparatus producing radiation come under the Ministry of Health and the Department of Health for Scotland. The monitoring of radioactive fallout is shared among the UKAEA, the Agricultural Research Council, and the Medical Research Council.

The siting of nuclear power stations, given the large dimensions of the projected long-range program and the small dimensions of the island, raises acute problems of safety, to say nothing of the perpetual concern to preserve the precious natural amenities of the countryside. Here, too, both the UKAEA and the Central Electricity Authority must rely on other agencies for the necessary authorizations. When, for example, the Harwell scientific establishment reached the optimum size compatible with efficiency of management and with the resources of the surrounding countryside, more than seventy sites had to be considered for the second establishment before settling on Winfreth Heath in Dorset. Many months of negotiation with the County Council followed, leading to a vote in council approving the application. There followed a public inquiry by the Ministry of Housing and Local Government, the ministry responsible for town and country planning in England and Wales. Ministerial approval was given, after consideration of all the evidence and subject to certain conditions governing layout, provision of screens of trees, and so forth. In addition to the natural local antipathy to the planning permission granted the authority, which threatened to mar wild heathland of exceptional beauty, there were legal complications arising from certain "commoners' rights" dating from the eighteenth century: part of the land had been set aside "for the preserving of furze, turf, and other fuells," and a special act of Parliament was necessary to override these claims.

The working conditions within plants operated by the authority are, like those in any industrial establishment, subject to regulation and inspection by the Factory Inspectorate of the Ministry of Labour. The authority has, in fact, gone to great lengths to protect its workers from both the special hazards of radiation and the more normal occupational risks associated with work in industry. Its health and safety record has been exemplary, and the elaborate records on radiation exposure maintained by the authority have shown no abnormal morbidity or mortality rates.

Effective regulation depends in part on an active research program as well as on the presence of a corps of persons properly trained in such relatively new fields as radiobiology, radiological physics, and radiophysiology. Following the report of a government committee (the Veale Committee), there has been a substantial expansion in special university courses in these fields, which should help overcome the current acute shortage of highly qualified personnel. It was this shortage of trained staff which induced the UKAEA to delay introduction of the previously mentioned Health and Safety Branch with comprehensive responsibility for safety standards and regulations.

In the conduct of research on health and safety hazards, which in turn provides the data for formulating regulatory standards, the authority works closely with the staffs of the Medical Research Council and the Agricultural Research Council. The former runs the Radiobiological Research Unit at Harwell, and its report, *The Hazards to Man of Nuclear and Allied Radiations,* is accepted by the authority as its standard for the control of radiation exposure. It is the two research councils, together with an advisory committee, who advise the responsible ministers on the levels of radioactivity to be prescribed for the disposal of atomic wastes. In practice, an exceedingly elaborate structure of advisory committees and interdepartmental committees has evolved to help in the task of keeping standards under constant review, and, on all these committees, the U.K. Atomic Energy Authority is represented.[9]

The gradual increase in the participation of non-governmental bodies in the nuclear-energy program necessitated the somewhat belated introduction of regulations to cover the non-governmental sector. In part, the legislation and regulations designed to cover the activities of the UKAEA were simply extended to cover the non-governmental participants. Two measures passed in 1959 established the new regulatory provisions. The Nuclear Installations (Licensing and Insurance) Act covered the disposal of radioactive wastes and also required the licensing of the construction and operation of nuclear reactors and any other such nuclear installations which might be prescribed by regulations. The licensing authority in England and Wales is the Ministry of Power, in Scotland, the Department of State, and in Northern Ireland, the Ministry of Commerce. These licensing authorities are empowered to impose whatever safety conditions they think fit to prescribe and to employ inspectors to assist in determining the conditions and seeing that regulations are being obeyed. The legislation lays down rather special insurance provisions to cover the liability of each licensee for injury or damage. Reflecting the unknown quality of the haz-

---

[9] Central Office of Information, *op. cit.,* pp. 43–48.

ards involved in exposure to radiation, the normal period of limitation (three years) has been raised to thirty years. Although the authority and other government departments are not themselves subject to the licensing provisions administered by their colleagues, they are subject to the same conditions covering liability.

A second measure, the Radioactive Substances Bill passed in the same year, was designed to cover users of radioactive substances who were not included in earlier legislation. All such users must be registered, and the accumulation or disposal of radioactive wastes by them must be in accordance with ministerial authorizations.

The paramount position of the Atomic Energy Authority in all the research and developmental aspects of the nuclear-energy program does not change the basic requirements for regulation and control, but it has influenced the nature of the organization designed to formulate and administer these regulations. The fact that the government has preserved a virtual monopoly of all materials, special fissile materials, and radioactive by-products such as isotopes has greatly diminished the necessity for regulatory action in these areas. Similarly, the predominance of the government, particularly in the early stages, in research and development meant that the basic issues with respect to regulatory standards for reactor safety, radiation hazards, and the like were worked out primarily within the authority itself, with a strong tendency to extend the jurisdiction of existing departments so as to cover the new field of atomic energy. By the time private participation in the program became significant, the standards and administrative controls already established to cover the state sector were simply carried over, virtually unchanged, to the private sector. Hence the Atomic Energy Authority, though very much involved in helping to formulate standards, has been concerned almost exclusively with ensuring that its own operating groups were complying with the standards. External inspection, as applied to its own and, more recently, to private installations, has been in the hands of ministries charged with the several aspects involved. Licensing of users and authorizations for construction and operation are not, therefore, a major feature of the authority's responsibilities as they are for the United States Atomic Energy Commission.

Canada. The Canadian arrangements for regulating the various activities associated with the nuclear-energy program differ, at least in formal design, from those adopted in either the United States or the United Kingdom. Canada has chosen to make a clear organizational separation between regulatory and operating activities. This formal separation has, in turn, led to a higher degree of concentration of authority for formulating regulations than exists elsewhere. But this concentration is modified in practice by the need, as in the United States, to achieve co-operative arrangements with the provinces in a federally organized state and the need to rely on existing departments to help administer the regulations. The fact that the government enjoys a quasi-monopolistic position with respect to certain parts of the atomic-energy program means that much regulation, as in Britain, is self-regulation.

The Atomic Energy Control Board was given, by the Act of 1946, supreme responsibility for formulating the regulations required in all areas of the nuclear-energy program. The Parliamentary debate touched off by the introduction of the legislation to create the board revealed much uncertainty about the particular responsibilities to be assumed by it.[10] The main question was whether it would be a strictly policy-making agency or whether, in addition, it would be responsible for operations. The statute itself was perfectly clear on this point: it conferred total and all-embracing powers on the board, making it responsible for research, the utilization of atomic energy, and the acquisition of mines, substances, and so on, as well as for the regulation of all aspects of the program.[11]

In actual practice, the Atomic Energy Control Board assumed only the regulatory responsibilities conferred on it, leaving

---

[10] "Fresh discoveries in the field of atomic energy may bring about swift developments which cannot now be foreseen precisely. Therefore, the measures for control must be not only wide, but also flexible, to meet the new situations." Mr. Howe, the minister in charge of the bill, in the House of Commons *Debates* (1946), p. 2108.

[11] *Statutes of Canada,* 10 Geo. VI, ch. 37.

operations and research to the National Research Council. These were subsequently transferred, in 1952, to Atomic Energy of Canada Ltd. In 1954, amending legislation brought the formal powers into line with actual practice.[12] The board became in law, as it had developed in fact, a glorified interagency committee responsible for formulating all nuclear-energy regulations and issuing permits and licenses required for the production and export of radioactive and source materials.

In discharging its manifold responsibilities, the board has relied on other departments regularly concerned with health and safety matters or on the other specialized bodies created to operate in the atomic-energy field. On the resources and materials side, private producers are required to obtain board permits for exploration and mining which allow them to drill, remove samples, and dispose of ores and concentrates. Prospectors and mining companies must provide the Geological Survey with data compiled in compliance with regulations of the board. But the key control is exerted by Eldorado Mining and Refining in its capacity as sole agent for the negotiation of contracts for the purchase and sale to foreign countries of ores, concentrates, precipitates, and products thereof produced in Canada.[13] The dependence of Canadian uranium producers on two foreign purchasers—the United States and the United Kingdom—"can be neatly fitted into the pattern long displayed by Canada's export staples," but the fact that such exports are allocated on the basis of intergovernmental agreements, which in turn are implemented by a governmental agency having a virtual monopoly of the supply, indicates the rigid nature of the controls exercised over source materials.[14] It further reveals the extreme dependence of the domestic controlling authority on decisions

[12] *Ibid.*, 2–3 Eliz. II, ch. 47.

[13] The sale of small quantities of uranium by private producers to countries falling outside the major contracts but having agreements with Canada has been permitted since 1958. India, West Germany, Japan, and Switzerland have been the largest purchasers, but this total in 1960 was less than .5 per cent of total exports. See W. D. G. Hunter, "The Development of the Canadian Uranium Industry: An Experiment in Public Enterprise," *The Canadian Journal of Economics and Political Science*, XXVIII (August, 1962), 348, Table III.

[14] *Loc. cit.*

taken outside its jurisdiction by powerful foreign purchasers.

Trading in prescribed substances is regulated by export and import permits issued by the Atomic Energy Control Board. Shipments of radioactive isotopes by Canadian suppliers, both for the domestic and foreign markets, must also be authorized by the board. But, once again, it is interesting to observe that the enforcement of the regulations is delegated to customs officials and to the staff of the Department of Trade and Commerce.

The board exercises its regulatory powers either by formulating general regulations or by issuing specific orders, licenses, or permits. General regulations define "prescribed substances," "prescribed equipment," and "protected places" and lay down conditions governing inspection, reporting, disclosure of information, patent rights, and many detailed requirements covering permissible exposure to radiation and the provision of necessary protective equipment.

In formulating these various regulations the board relies, as does the United States Atomic Energy Commission, on numerous advisory committees. For example, health and safety standards covering the handling of radioactive materials were recently revised with the help of a drafting committee which worked closely with the Dominion Council of Health and the provincial and federal departments of health. Administration of the regulations developed in this way has been delegated to the respective provincial and federal departments of health.[15]

Similarly, the Reactor Safety Advisory Committee, which reports to the president of Atomic Energy of Canada Ltd., is the board's agency for reviewing and making recommendations on the design and operation of reactors. This committee ensures that the health and safety requirements laid down in the board's reactor construction permits are met. All persons using radioactive materials are subject to the board's regulations, which once again are administered by safety officers in the federal Department of Health and Welfare and, through them, by their provincial counterparts. As in the United States, the development of appropriate health standards and the devolution of

---

[15] See *Annual Report of the Atomic Energy Control Board for the Year 1959–60* (Ottawa: Queen's Printer, 1960), for details on these negotiations.

their enforcement to the provinces has necessitated more than the usually prolonged discussion which attends any administrative matter that cuts across dominion-provincial jurisdiction. Only in the last year or two has a satisfactory modus vivendi been worked out—although Canada may have achieved an earlier success at devolution than has the United States, which is still grappling with the problem.

Since the government's operating role is proportionately more significant and therefore more akin to the situation in the United Kingdom than the United States, it is not surprising to find that a heavy burden for ensuring safety and proper health arrangements has been placed on the government's own operator, Atomic Energy of Canada Ltd. In fact, within its own establishment, the company has created three divisions which constitute the major repository of specialized scientific knowledge about radiation hazards and reactor safety arrangements. A small Reactor Commissioning Division supplements the work of the previously mentioned Reactor Safety Advisory Committee. A Biology and Health Physics Division carries out applied research and development on improved safety and warning devices, performs basic research on the biological effects of ionizing radiations and the use of radioactive isotopes, and provides technical advice to other government departments, private industry, the armed services, and the universities. Finally, the Medical Division assumes responsibility for advising and training management and supervising the administration of all safety precautions within the company's own plants. This division is also represented on a number of advisory committees and international bodies.

It is to be observed that the formal separation of the agency responsible for regulation from other bodies concerned with the application of nuclear energy does not, in practice, produce results that differ much from the experience of the countries previously reviewed. Administration or enforcement of the regulations, as in the United Kingdom, tends to fall on other departments or agencies. And, in the formulation of regulations, the board probably has to rely, much more than the United States or Britain, on the expert knowledge and advice of the government agency most directly involved in operations and development. The fact is that Canada has fewer organizations outside the government to which it can turn for such scientific and technical advice. Also, like the United States, Canada has had to develop its regulatory apparatus with full regard to the requirements of a federal system.

France. The production of nuclear materials in France is governed essentially by the same laws and rules that are applicable to the more conventional mining and fabricating enterprises; these regulations are enforced primarily by government agencies having a traditional responsibility for such matters. It is important to note, however, that the French Atomic Energy Authority has been directly involved in a major way in preliminary explorations and in the mining and processing of the ores and, as a consequence, is itself subjected to the regulations which also apply to private entrepreneurs. Control is exercised by means of permits and concessions available equally to individuals and to companies. Preliminary exploration and test drilling can be carried out, provided that a declaration of intent has been made to the chief engineer for mines. A permit is required if substantial capital investment and works are contemplated, and this in turn can be followed up by the grant of an exclusive concession to develop the mine, after satisfactory evidence of financial and technical capacity has been provided. Exploitation permits are granted by decree of the minister for mines, acting on the advice of the governing board of the Atomic Energy Authority. Each permit is good for five years and is renewable for two additional five-year periods. Mining concessions to holders of exclusive permits can be granted by the Council of State (Conseil d'État), acting again on the advice of the authority.

The customary surveillance of safety conditions in the mines is performed by inspectors from the Department of Mines, who are assisted by the staff of the Atomic Energy Authority. Full information is required from all concerned with mining of source materials. All nuclear substances must be sold to the Atomic Energy Authority, and, although the authority is buttressed by the power to expropriate, it has never been necessary to exercise the power in order to maintain control over supplies.

The foregoing requirements, though directed particularly to private persons and companies, are equally applicable to the authority. Indeed, until about 1955, the exploration for and exploitation of the raw materials were conducted almost entirely by the authority under permits and concessions granted by the responsible government authorities. By the end of 1955, however, private parties were operating with fifteen exploration permits and five exploitation permits, covering a total area of two thousand eight hundred square kilometers.

Before attaining their independence in 1958, the French overseas territories were governed by regulations closely paralleling those in force in metropolitan France, and very little alteration has occurred since independence. By virtue of co-operative agreements concluded with Senegal, Gabon, the Congo, Madagascar, and the Central African Republic, a common policy for regulating the use of sttrategic primary materials has been formulated.

Two series of measures embrace the trade in source and special nuclear materials and in the apparatus directly employed in the development of nuclear energy. One set of measures, primarily economic in character, relates to prohibited goods, for which export and import licenses must be obtained. The other set covers a limited number of strategic materials, as defined by NATO, which are designed to restrict trade to members of the organization. For these, a rigorous system of export and import certificates is in effect. Additional regulations are imposed by virtue of the government's participation in EURATOM and the Organization for European Co-operation and Development.

The production of all radioactive isotopes is virtually monopolized by the Atomic Energy Authority and their domestic use is strictly regulated under the Public Health Code. Industrial users must first make a declaration before the mayor or, in Paris, the prefect of police. Their medical use is also subject to strict control by the Ministry of Public Health for therapeutic or biological research purposes, radioactive exposure, and the like. In 1954 changes in the legislation made the authority responsible for regulating the trade in these elements and subjected certain users to special authorizations granted by an Interdepartmental Committee on Radioactive Isotopes. The chairman of this committee or the president of the council must authorize exports for other than medical uses or any transfer of such radioactive substances. These regulations do not apply to radioactive products manufactured by the authority, but transfers of these must be approved by the interdepartmental committee.

No special regulations have been issued to cover the disposal of atomic wastes, but the general rules applying to industry prevent the ejection of any industrial wastes which might imperil public health and safety, and there are similar prohibitions applying to noxious emissions into water, public drains, and the air. The only legislation applying specifically to radioactive pollution was approved in August, 1961, and dealt only with atmospheric contamination. This problem of waste disposal will undoubtedly become more serious as the nuclear-energy program gains momentum. The abortive effort of the authority in 1960 to bury its wastes in the Mediterranean raised such a storm of protest from coastal dwellers that the plan had to be abandoned. Elsewhere, at Marcoule for example, the wastes are treated and the residues buried underground. Public opinion in France, as elsewhere, is easily aroused over hazards to health, and it is likely that the special regulations imposed will, as in other countries, show an excess of caution in order to reassure the public.

Finally, in the matter of regulating the siting, construction, and safe operation of nuclear reactors, we find a reliance, similar to that in the United Kingdom and Canada, on internal self-regulation. Three divisions attached to the high commissioner's office in the authority provide the research data and technical and inspection staff required to formulate and apply the standards to the operating units of the authority. Basic research is conducted by the Biology Division, the protection of workers against radiation hazards is undertaken by the Atomic Hygiene and Radiopathology Division and by the Division for Control of Radiation and Radiation Engineering. These essentially internal regulatory services are performed in close co-operation with the Ministry of Public Health.

The private persons and firms engaged in the construction of reactors are subjected to existing legislation and regulations, suitably expanded to include the new threats to health and safety posed by atomic energy. Establishments which constitute a threat to security and health are graded into three categories, according to the degree of danger presented by their operation, their proximity to settled communities and their likely impact on their physical surroundings. Regulations for the lower order of risks are imposed by the prefects of the respective *departements.* Those in the other categories must seek permission to embark on construction by first submitting to a public inquiry. In addition, under the Urban and Housing Code, construction permits must be obtained by private persons and all public services; permits are issued by the prefect or sometimes by the Ministry for Construction. The scientific as well as the industrial establishments of the Atomic Energy Authority are equally subject to regulations designed to implement a general policy of industrial decentralization. A special regulatory procedure, known as *l'instruction mixte,* is followed wherever mines, factories, or other installations designed to produce radioactive or fissile materials for thermonuclear reactors are involved.

In short, the major features of the regulatory arrangements in France show a striking similarity to the British system. There is the same reliance on internal controls provided by divisions within the authority and necessitated by the enormous dimensions of the authority's own establishments. There is also the same resort to other departments to formulate and administer the regulations—going farther in the case of France because the authority itself is bound by most of these regulations.

Japan. Regulation of the entire nuclear-energy program in Japan is characterized by extremely detailed prescriptions covering every eventuality and incorporated in statutes, cabinet orders, and numerous regulations, all founded on the organic act of 1955. The country's direct experience with the devastating impact of the first bombs undoubtedly accounts for the early efforts to enshrine the maximum security and precautionary measures in a detailed regulatory code. Moreover, in the immediate postwar period, the occupying powers made it clear that once Japan embarked on its own nuclear-energy program, only the peaceful applications could be developed. Hence, in addition to the inherent health and safety factors calling for regulation, there was the need to assure the international community that strict control existed to forestall any military applications.[16] This combination of intense domestic concern for adequate precautions and the occupying powers' general interest in encouraging only peaceful applications accounts for the unique role thrust on the prime minister in formulating and supervising the enforcement of regulations. The prime minister, usually in conjunction with the Ministry of International Trade and Industry and the Atomic Energy Commission, must give his formal approval to a wide range of detailed activities relating to every aspect of the nuclear-energy program.

In the first instance, nuclear source materials (carefully defined in the law and regulations) are subject to close control. Materials need not necessarily be owned by the government, but their use or transfer is subject to authorizations issued by the prime minister or the minister of international trade and industry. All enriched uranium, imported mainly under the bilateral agreement with the United States, has to be held by the government. All reprocessing of fuels is also in the hands of the government's Atomic Fuel Corporation.

Concerns other than the Atomic Fuel Corporation who wish to embark on a refinery business must seek the approval of the prime minister, as does any private fabricator. The Fuel Corporation, which is the government's refining and fabricating agency, undertakes the major part of these activities. It is required to maintain detailed records for scrutiny by the Prime Minister's Office or the Ministry of International Trade and Industry. The corporation is responsible for all safety regulations within its establishments, but their terms are approved, as are any changes, by the same two high offices.

All private concerns planning to construct and operate

---

[16] In 1961, an amendment to the Regulation of Nuclear Source Material, Nuclear Fuel Material and Atomic Reactors Act, 1957, codified the obligations imposed by international agreements.

nuclear reactors must seek permission from the same sources. The Japan Atomic Energy Research Institute, as the central governmental body concerned with nuclear reactor research and development, must also apply to the Prime Minister's Office for approval of design and method of construction; subsequently, these facilities are subject to inspection and performance evaluation. Once in operation, reactors used for power generation must submit their plans of operation for the approval of the Prime Minister's Office and the Ministry of International Trade and Industry; when the reactor is to be placed in a ship, approval of the Ministry of Transport must be obtained.

Thus far the problem of regulating the disposal of radioactive wastes has not been particularly pressing, for these have been associated almost entirely with the production of radioisotopes. Currently, these wastes are collected and stored by the Japan Radioactivity Association, a private body which is subsidized by the government in the performance of this essential service. Clearly, as the nation's atomic program expands, a public organization will have to assume full responsibility for this activity.

The use and sale of radioisotopes and the use of all apparatus involving radiation hazards are subject to special legislation.[17] The director general of the Science and Technics Agency is primarily responsible for enforcing the regulations by means of "certificates of permission." The regulations themselves are promulgated either by the Prime Minister's Office or, in the case of transportation by conventional means, by the Ministry of Transport.

The original enactment provided for the creation of a Radiation Council within the Science and Technics Agency to advise the director general in the performance of his regulatory functions. A subsequent statute, approved in 1958, placed the council "as an affiliated organ" (Art. 4) in the Prime Minister's Office and specified that the council "shall make research and deliberate on" technical standards for prevention of radiation hazards and measurement of radiation. The council is a part-time

---

[17] Law Concerning Prevention of Radiation Hazards Due to Radioactive Isotopes etc., Law No. 167, June 10, 1957.

body composed of government representatives and outsiders "with learning and experience in the prevention of radiation hazards" (Art. 6).[18]

In addition to these governmental arrangements for formulating and administering regulations, there is the Japan Science Council which represents the voice of university scientists and is, therefore, an independent, expert, and sometimes critical commentator on the government's regulatory policies. In particular, it has acted as a conservative counterweight to any temptation which a governmental agency concerned with operations as well as regulations might have to cut corners or run unnecessary risks in its reactor-development policy. In fact, as in other countries, the weight of public opinion has quite successfully imposed on the government a conservative approach to such matters.

Clearly, the powers conferred on the Prime Minister's Office to develop and enforce the regulations described above cannot be exercised without scientific and technical support from competent agencies concerned with the nuclear-energy program. In the first instance, this advice and information are expected to come from the Atomic Energy Commission; Article 2 (iv) of the Law for the Establishment of the Atomic Energy Commission states that "the regulation of nuclear fuel materials and reactors" shall be among the many matters on which the commission "shall plan, deliberate and decide." But, for this task, the Commission is also empowered to "ask for the presentation of data, expressions of opinion, explanation, or any other necessary cooperation from the chiefs of administrative government organs concerned" (Art. 5).

In practice, the commission acts essentially as a device for co-ordinating and formulating the technical advice coming up from the operating agencies and placing this before the prime minister for approval. The agencies primarily involved are the Science and Technics Agency, particularly its Atomic Energy Bureau, and the Japan Atomic Energy Research Institute. Within the latter agency, a committee for the examination of

---

[18] Law Concerning Technical Standards for Prevention of Radiation Hazards, Law No. 162, May 21, 1958.

reactor safety has been set up to render special advice on all matters pertaining to the siting, construction, and operation of nuclear reactors. In this respect, Japan follows close on the heels of other countries in vesting responsibility for regulation in the agency which is also concerned with promotion and development. As yet, the internal organizational separation which is a distinctive and deliberate development in both the United States and Britain has not evolved. But it is interesting to observe that in its *Long-Range Program on Development and Utilization of Atomic Energy,* the Japan Atomic Energy Commission comments that "it will be necessary for the AEC's Safety Examination Committee to be reconstituted into an independent and permanent committee distinct from other committees so that its functions may be strengthened." [19]

The administrative arrangements for regulating atomic energy in Japan are unique in the amount of responsibility formally conferred on the Prime Minister's Office—in its detail, going well beyond the powers conferred on the chief executives of other countries. In practice, however, the prime minister has been provided with an ample supporting structure, attached directly to his office or reporting to him; thus, he does not lack for the technical or scientific advice so necessary in regulating this new and rapidly expanding field.

Italy. The organization for regulating and administering the atomic-energy program in Italy is still at a formative state. The shortened nuclear law of 1960 not only clarified and strengthened the position of the National Committee for Nuclear Energy but, among other objectives, declared its purpose to be the maintenance of a scientific and technical supervision over all activities connected with the use of source and fissile materials, the production of nuclear energy, and the use of all equipment and materials in plants and laboratories. This general supervisory authority is, however, substantially curtailed for all practical purposes by the strong voice accorded existing departments having responsibilities which embrace one or more

---

[19] Japan, Atomic Energy Commission, *Long-Range Program on Development and Utilization of Atomic Energy* (February 8, 1961), p. 127.

aspects of the atomic-energy program. In particular, the close identification with the Ministry of Industry and Commerce is likely to create difficulties for the committee in its dealings with other departments that also have a strong interest in the non-industrial aspects of the program. A closer tie with the Prime Minister's Office, comparable to that established in Japan, would appear to provide a more viable arrangement for strengthening the status and independence of the committee.

Turning to the specific elements of the atomic-energy program which have to be regulated, we find that nuclear source materials are covered under a royal decree of July 29, 1927, the so-called Mines Law. This enactment provides that all minerals are state owned and subjects exploration to state permission and extraction to a government concession. The enactment of 1962 on atomic energy envisages a broadening of the High Council for Mines by the inclusion of a representative of the National Committee for Nuclear Energy and proposes to compel all those holding any significant quantity of metallic uranium or other source materials to declare their property.

Domestic trade in these materials or radioactive substances requires a permit from the Ministry of Industry and Commerce, assuming that EURATOM does not exercise its option to regulate under Article 57 of the founding Treaty of Rome. The same treaty also provides that the community shall own all special nuclear materials (Art. 86). The Ministry of Foreign Commerce, in agreement with the Ministry for Industry and Commerce, issues the necessary export and import permits, as well as authorizing the transport of fissionable or radioactive materials.[20]

The delay in achieving legislative support for a detailed code of regulations has produced a rather confused situation in which the parties involved have had to rely on fair play and, to some extent, on the pervasive influence of the regulations which Italy accepted in joining EURATOM. Clearly, the regulations imposed by numerous local authorities, designed to cover more conventional substances dangerous to the public, are not ade-

---

[20] The detailed regulatory provisions discussed here are based on the enlarged version of the Atomic Energy Act, the second part of which in amended form was approved December 31, 1962.

quate to meet the special hazards of nuclear substances. Rigorous national control is required, and the recent nationalization of electricity, which will at least place all nuclear-power reactors under state control, should permit the development of self-regulation which has been common in the other countries reviewed.

The enactment of 1962 also makes provision for a rigorous control over the use of radioactive isotopes. Industrial users will have to obtain permits from the Ministry of Industry and Commerce; the Health Ministry will issue the necessary authorizations for diagnostic and therapeutic uses, the Ministry of Agriculture for agricultural uses, and the Ministry of Public Education for didactic purposes. Scientific institutions are to be exempted, but the minister of industry and commerce may promulgate detailed regulations covering the general use of radioisotopes.

Nuclear reactors and installations are also to be subjected to firm national controls. The Ministry of Industry and Commerce must authorize all applications for construction of a nuclear power plant, such applications to be accompanied by full documentation detailing the features of the plant and its safety devices. These applications are subjected to the same kind of "hazards evaluation" as is employed by the United States Atomic Energy Commission. In this case, the National Committee on Nuclear Energy provides the ministry with the technical evaluation. Until the enactment of 1962, this regulatory system had been applied only to siting and plans; no provision for regulating actual construction or operation of the plants had been formulated. However, with the first power reactors under construction and scheduled for completion in 1963, the new measure of 1962 fills this gap in the regulatory apparatus.

Since Italy has no plants for fabricating uranium or other material for reactor cores, the state is able to exert a significant control over plant builders who have to rely on government-supplied fuel. This fuel, in turn, is procured by the government under international agreements which require the recipient to maintain adequate control over the ultimate destination of the fuels and their safe employment. Under these circumstances, the government can insist on proper construction standards and adequate safety precautions being met as a condition for the delivery of the fuel. The government's regulatory role is further supported by the transition from informal authorizations to a system of more formal concessions which has the effect of stressing the public-interest features which are so dominant in the peaceful development and application of nuclear energy. A special procedure is required to issue the concessions: a committee of ministers, backed by the expert advice of the National Committee for Nuclear Energy, makes the decisions. The concession, which is for a maximum of twenty years, lays down conditions as to siting, disposal of wastes, cost and amount of time required to build the plant, financial guarantees—including civil liability to third parties—and other conditions relating to public safety. The actual construction of the plant can be controlled by the Ministry of Industry and Commerce, which is empowered to set up a test commission for the purpose. Only after the test commission and the National Committee for Nuclear Energy report favorably does the minister authorize operation of the plant.

The legislation of 1962 also envisages a system of operating licenses for nuclear plants used either for power generation or for naval propulsion. In the latter instance, the bill proposes that the president of the republic should undertake to formulate the rules governing the operation of nuclear-propelled ships, acting on the advice of the minister of merchant shipping, in agreement with the ministers of defense and industry and commerce.

In general, then, it can be said that regulations already existing in Italy and confirmed or extended in the 1962 legislative enactment envisage a tight regimen of controls comparable to those already more fully developed and in use elsewhere. Much the same problem of co-ordinating a variety of existing departments already occupying one or more of the areas embraced by atomic energy has arisen. The greater dispersion of regulatory powers and the relatively weak position of the National Committee for Nuclear Energy suggests that co-ordination will be much more difficult to accomplish in the Italian setting.

International Regulation. One of the first steps taken by the newly constituted United Nations was to set up a special committee to explore the possibility of devising an organization for regulating nuclear energy on an international basis. Since the awesome destructive capacity of the atom was of immediate concern to all nations, early efforts to create a regulatory mechanism were directed to "internationalizing" the military elements of the nuclear-energy program. It became increasingly apparent that these efforts were premature, and the high optimism of the negotiators was soon reduced to a dogged pursuit of more limited objectives.

In the interval, however, much more success has attended the efforts to achieve international and regional control over the peaceful applications of nuclear energy. If the special attributes of nuclear energy called for rigorous regulation of its domestic applications, they equally called for specialized regulatory agencies transcending national boundaries. The capacity to use nuclear materials and products for both warlike and peaceful purposes necessitated some supranational regulatory apparatus to ensure that these were not diverted to purposes incompatible with the objectives for which the international or regional agencies had been created. Moreover, insofar as research and development were taken up by groups of states, it was necessary to offset the hazards to health and security arising from the use of radioactive materials, construction and operation of nuclear reactors, transshipment of fissionable materials, pollution of air and water, and so on.

The parallel between the domestic and international necessity for regulation can be extended to the formulation and administration of the regulations. Just as each nation has faced problems of co-ordinating the efforts of the atomic energy agency with those of conventional departments having a concern for one or more aspects of the program, so, too, the same problems arise at the supranational level. A comment on each of these aspects of the regulatory process will help to reinforce the obvious similarities of national and international problems and objectives.

The original, ill-starred proposal offered by the United

States to the United Nations Commission on Atomic Energy would have given the projected International Atomic Development Authority control throughout the world of all dangerous, i.e., military, applications of atomic energy. National and private activities were to have been restricted, subject to control by the authority, to peaceful research and the operation of power reactors. International tensions forestalled this plan and, in a sense, led to its reversal: military applications were kept very much under the exclusive jurisdiction of each nation, and only those peaceful elements which the individual nations agreed to assign to supranational authorities were brought under broader jurisdictions. Had the nations agreed to one plan proposed for the International Atomic Energy Agency established in 1957, they would, in fact, have made available to that agency such significant quantities of special fissionable materials to be used for peaceful purposes that their war-making potential would have been effectively and equitably curtailed. Unfortunately, the negotiators had to settle for a much more modest arrangement which left the nuclear powers quite unhampered in continuing the arms race.

Ideally, then, as long as fissionable materials can be used for war or for peace, international control depends on placing the source materials beyond the reach of individual nations. In practice, the nations have been unwilling to concede anything like this much power to an international body. The statute of the International Atomic Energy Agency, the EURATOM Treaty, and the Security Control Convention relating to the European Nuclear Energy Agency all contain provisions whereby certain peaceful activities of the member states can be supervised by the respective organizations in order to ensure that no diversion of material or effort to military use will result. The EURATOM Treaty goes farther in that all activities of or in the member states, except those declared to be military, are supervised by the agency. The other two supranational authorities are limited to supervising those activities which may be assisted by them or which have been voluntarily submitted to their control. Influence and persuasion, rather than directly delegated powers, play a prominent part in the operations of these agencies.

Supranational authorities are not alone in having to contend with the ambivalent nature of the atom. In the United States, Britain, and France, where the nuclear-energy program is devoted to both peaceful and warlike applications, the agency primarily responsible for atomic energy is either excluded from the strictly military aspects of the program or is required to act on an agency basis for the armed services; the latter may even conduct much of the research and development work themselves. In this respect, the domestic situation does not differ greatly from the separation between military and peaceful applications which has been made for purposes of supranational control.

This segregation, coupled with a limited delegation of authority to supervise certain aspects of the peaceful nuclear-energy program, limits but certainly does not eliminate the possibility of achieving positive results from supranational regulatory bodies. The most significant of these relate to the formulation and enforcement of standards governing safety and health. The procedure followed by the International Atomic Energy Agency in devising such standards may serve as an illustration. The secretariat of the agency develops a preliminary set of standards which is submitted to an expert panel representing a number of member states in various stages of development and with different problems and legal systems. Representatives from interested non-governmental and intergovernmental organizations are also included. If further scientific information is required, the agency undertakes to obtain the information through research contracts with outside firms, through its own facilities or through the facilities of the member states. Ultimately, a draft set of regulations is circulated and, if the subject is important, goes before the board of the agency for approval. These are the standards which then become operative whenever the agency makes agreements to provide financial or other assistance to the atomic-energy programs of individual states. Member states and other international bodies are invited to incorporate these standards into their own regulations—and frequently do.

As the peaceful applications of atomic energy are extended, more and more problems of a transnational character require the attention of an international regulatory body. Pollution of international waters by the expected early introduction of nuclear-propelled vessels and pollution of the air or waters by atomic wastes or by accidents to nuclear reactors demand international monitoring and a common code of regulations. The increasing flow of international trade in radioactive and fissionable substances similarly necessitates the adoption and enforcement of common regulations. Formulation of liability conventions to facilitate trade in such dangerous substances or to ensure uniform standards with respect to insurable limits for adjudicating claims is already under way: the European Nuclear Energy Agency has already developed a convention covering such matters, and a world-wide convention dealing with reactors on land and in ships is now being formulated with the assistance of the International Atomic Energy Agency.

Neither the International Atomic Energy Agency nor the regional organizations is able to operate—any more than their national counterparts—without reference to other agencies whose jurisdictions partially embrace the nuclear-energy field. The World Health Organization is concerned, for example, with radiation safety and with the medical use of isotopes; it currently collects and publishes legislation dealing with radiation safety. The International Labour Organization is similarly interested in the protection of workers from radiation. The Food and Agriculture Organization uses isotopes for agricultural research and development, while UNESCO is responsible for encouraging the development and exchange of scientific information. The International Maritime Consultative Organization, in the 1960 revision of its Convention for Safety of Life at Sea, incorporated appropriate provisions to deal with nuclear-propelled ships. The International Civil Aviation Organization and the Universal Postal Union have a similar concern for the safe transport of nuclear materials. The World Meteorological Organization is responsible for the monitoring of environmental radioactivity, primarily in the atmosphere. Finally, the specialized agencies attached to regional organizations also have interests that have to be related to those of the regional atomic-energy authorities. In short, the existence of specialized organs for regulating the peaceful uses of atomic energy pose the need, both domestically and internationally, for constant co-ordination and co-operation with the agencies in charge of conventional power and related matters of health or safety.

Summary and Conclusion. Several conclusions emerge from the foregoing comments on the regulatory practices and procedures of individual countries and of international or regional agencies responsible for developing the peaceful uses of atomic energy. First, it is clear that the substances and processes used are sufficiently unique to require especially rigorous control measures. Nevertheless, a functional administrative arrangement which singles out one source of energy for special attention cannot help but run athwart the conventional organization of departments by major purpose—health, labor, agriculture, trade, and so on. At least two important administrative problems are thereby created. The most obvious is the acute need to co-ordinate the regulatory activities of the specialized atomic-energy agencies with the policing powers long held by the regular departments.

The second problem is that the specialized nuclear-energy agency may be involved in an operational or promotional role as well as a regulatory role. In countries like the United States and the United Kingdom, where the two activities are to a large extent combined, they have been segregated into separate divisions within the agency. Elsewhere—in Canada, for example —although the organizational form adopted may suggest a clearer distinction, the practice is to involve the operating agency closely with the regulatory body. It would therefore appear that whether or not there is a physical separation of the agencies responsible for operations and for regulation, the need for extremely close collaboration between the two, especially at the early stages, has been fully acknowledged by most countries.

The critical point is not so much the propriety of blending two separate and superficially incompatible functions, but the determination of how and by whom the regulations themselves should be framed. Although the matters which are comprehended by the regulations are technical and scientific in substance, in the final analysis, the main guide lines must be based on political rather than scientific criteria. The determination of the appropriate safety level for radiation exposure is susceptible to scientific analysis, but the final definition is probably about as variable as the definition of "pure" water for drinking purposes: we can no more achieve absolute safety in an atomic-energy establishment or in the handling of radioactive materials than we can obtain absolutely pure water. But we can adopt a "permissible" dosage—an acceptable standard based on a balance of risks, costs, public expectations, and the administrative capabilities of the agencies concerned with enforcement. The scientist can contribute his quota of expert knowledge and advice to the formulation, but the over-all balance is not determined by scientific analysis alone. It is for this reason that final determinations in this area are generally left to a higher political authority. In the United States, for example, this authority is the president himself, and the compromise character of the decisions he makes is partially indicated by the widely representative Federal Radiation Council which advises him; in Japan, it is the prime minister, and elsewhere it is the cabinet or a responsible minister—all acting in close consultation with the experts engaged on the operational-promotional side of the atomic-energy program.

The matter of determining the appropriate authority for making regulations in a field as complex as atomic energy is not easily settled. It raises a fundamental question about the relation between the interested expert and the responsible lay politician. For the moment, it must be concluded that if, indeed, the amateur is to be vested with final authority to make these decisions, he must have access to the broadest possible range of technical opinion and scientific advice. On this score, it would appear that most national authorities, as well as regional and international agencies, have managed to surround themselves with the necessary governmental or non-governmental advisors capable of rendering this essential service to the decision-makers.

Finally, it may be asked, to what extent has it been necessary for the state to assume operating responsibilities as a means of maintaining control over the several facets of the atomic-energy program? In practice, because of the war-engendered origins of atomic energy and the continued possibility of turning the materials to warlike purposes, all states have taken the easiest way out by insisting on preserving a monopoly of the fissionable materials. In the absence of comprehensive international regulation, it is likely that this direct method of control will be retained. However, it is questionable that the state need preserve a monopoly of the mining, refining, processing, and fabrication in order to maintain complete surveillance over fissionable substances.

It is equally clear that the more the state devolves to private hands the various research, developmental, and commercial applications of nuclear energy, the more complex the problem of regulation will become. The United States, which has gone farther in this devolution than any other country surveyed, has a more difficult regulatory situation to contend with than do those countries in which the bulk of operations is still in governmental hands. For the latter, regulation becomes essentially a matter of developing internal control arrangements and modifying and extending these where necessary to embrace the limited group of private participants. There is always the danger, in such circumstances, that internal regulations may be drafted with too firm an eye on the operating necessities of the state atomic-energy agencies. The safeguard would appear to lie in conferring powers to formulate and enforce the regulations on departments that already have comprehensive regulatory powers over such matters as health, construction, and working conditions. The atomic-energy agency will, of course, have to be given a voice in the decisions reached by these other authorities, but it should not be given a position of pre-eminence simply because it carries the main operating burdens.

VII
Co-ordination

The decision to segregate one portion of a nation's scientific and developmental effort and to create special organs to implement the program has given rise to numerous problems of co-ordination. First, there is the problem of bringing the atomic-energy program into balance with the total scientific and promotional activities of the nation. Second, there is the area of regulation which, as the previous chapter makes abundantly clear, cuts across the jurisdiction of existing departments which have traditional regulatory powers in closely related fields. Finally, in the vast governmental organizations specifically designed to administer the atomic-energy program, there is a need to evolve machinery that can co-ordinate the disparate parts of the program. The characteristic features of the co-ordinating devices developed to meet these problems may best be evaluated by examining the practices of the countries selected for this survey.

The United States. The situation in the United States provides an excellent illustration of the co-ordinating problems posed when an organization is formed around one source of energy in opposition to the tradition of organizing around a major function. In these circumstances, the programs and responsibilities of the regular departments and agencies inevitably impinge on those assigned to the Atomic Energy Commission.

The need to consult and to collaborate is most strikingly felt in the many regulatory activities shared between the commission and other departments. The problem has been met by using advisory committees representing various interested governmental agencies as well as outside experts. Some of these, notably the General Advisory Committee to the commission, are permanent; others are *ad hoc*.[1]

For research and development, the establishment of co-operative projects has helped to overcome some of the overlapping and duplication. The nuclear rocket program sponsored jointly by the Atomic Energy Commission and the National Aeronautics and Space Administration is the outstanding example of such a device. Co-ordination is also furthered by the commission's method of financing projects undertaken by other agencies. The Science Information Exchange Service of the Smithsonian Institution has also been of great assistance in keeping various agencies informed about work in related fields, thereby preventing obvious duplication of research.

Useful as these devices are, they do not solve the key jurisdictional problems arising from overlapping assignments, and in the last analysis the only feasible way of settling disputes has been to make the president responsible for final policy decisions and organizational questions. The fact that the executive pyramid tapers off sharply to the lone figure of the president lends a superficial unity of command and organization which the cabinet systems of Britain and Canada, for instance, cannot display. On the other hand, because all these matters come to one person who has ultimate political responsibility, he must rely heavily on an efficient staff. The most important of these is the Bureau of the Budget, and, since most interagency conflicts arise in a budgetary or organizational context, the skilled services of the bureau are deployed to bring about a reconciliation of policy objectives or organizational conflicts. When the bureau fails, the personal intervention of the president is required. But even at this point the president is not free to act autonomously, for the separation of powers in the United States always provides the disgruntled agency with an alternative court of appeal, Congress. In the case of atomic energy, the unique Joint Committee on Atomic Energy has forced the president to share his executive prerogatives in an almost unprecedented fashion.

---

[1] Consult Don K. Price, *Government and Science* ("Galaxy Book," [New York: Oxford University Press, 162]), especially "The Machinery of Advice."

The emergence of the specialized international or regional atomic-energy bodies has added another dimension to the problem of domestic co-ordination. Agencies like the International Atomic Energy Agency and EURATOM have, to some extent, taken over some of the co-ordination, but, since President Eisenhower's atoms-for-peace policy was enunciated in 1953, the increasing involvement of the United States in international programs has raised new problems at home. Where, for example, should responsibility for the United States' share of this program be placed? This question brought the Atomic Energy Commission and the International Cooperation Administration (operating under the Department of State) into direct collision in 1956. Should the agency with the greatest technical competency as well as the statutory authority for developing the peaceful uses of atomic energy be placed in charge? Or was this a matter primarily of foreign policy and, consequently, a matter for the International Cooperation Administration? Ultimately a compromise was reached, leaving the program in the hands of the Commission but according the Department of State a large advisory role in all foreign-policy aspects.[2] This far from clear-cut solution is typical of the untidy organizational responsibility that has evolved for most of the areas in which the commission is only one of a number of agencies sharing an interest in a particular aspect of the nuclear-energy program.

The United Kingdom. The United Kingdom Atomic Energy Authority presides over one of the largest single scientific enterprises in the world. For this reason it faces a problem of co-ordinating which has its parallels elsewhere, but perhaps not of the same dimensions. Since April, 1961, one of the members of the governing board of the authority has been designated deputy chairman and assigned the responsibility of co-ordinating all technical and scientific work. In addition, on each of the management boards of the five groups of the authority sit representatives from the central board and each of the respective groups. The

---

[2] For additional comments on this problem, see William H. Berman and Lee M. Hydeman, "Atomic Energy Policy Review," *Bulletin of the Atomic Scientists*, XVIII (March 1962), 35–37.

London office acts as a co-ordinating center for negotiating with various ministries on the policies and finances of the authority. This co-ordinating mechanism has been criticized for being top-heavy,[3] and the widely dispersed organizations have had to be further co-ordinated by relying on an unusually large number of committees, to which scientists seem as much addicted as regular bureaucrats.[4]

The overlapping jurisdiction in regulatory action which is the inevitable consequence of conferring special organizational status on atomic energy is handled by *ad hoc* and permanent committees. On all of these committees, the Atomic Energy Authority is represented, but by no means plays a leading role. Because a large portion of the program is conducted in the authority's establishments, much of the regulation can be co-ordinated by internal mechanisms.

For the co-ordination of the over-all scientific programs and policies and the balancing of the special requirements of the nuclear-energy program, several mechanisms are employed. The key official is the minister for science, a portfolio created in 1959. He is responsible for the general oversight of all space research, all the work of a number of government-sponsored research councils, and all government scientific research except defense research. For all practical purposes, he is the "minister for atomic energy." Half of his small office consists of the staff of the Atomic Energy Division, and through this office he exercises his statutory responsibility for ensuring that "in the affairs of the [UKAEA] the proper degrees of importance are attached to the various applications of atomic energy." His statutory powers of direction extend beyond the issuance of general directions (familiar to all nationalized industries) to the power to issue "such directions as he may think fit." In fact, the general policy framework within which the authority is required to operate has been rather clearly outlined for such important matters as production

---

[3] *The Economist,* March 25, 1961, p. 1217.

[4] In 1957, the then Industrial Group had 150 committees. Subsequently, these were pared down to thirty-five, but one senior executive of the group had to attend 106 committee meetings a year. Members of the governing board in London attended fourteen of the thirty-five committees—and this for only one group.

of fissile material and the objectives of the civil power program. Very early, there was a formal directive forbidding the authority to embark on any undertaking having international implications without first referring to the official Interdepartmental Committee on Nuclear Energy and, if need be, through that body to the Cabinet Committee on Atomic Energy.

The regular annual budgetary review, as in the United States, is also a convenient instrument of co-ordination. In the case of the Atomic Energy Authority, this review is more rigorous than that applied to the regular nationalized industries because most of its funds must be appropriated. These funds are voted by Parliament to the Ministry of Science, not directly to the Authority, and it is the minister who must account to the legislature for their use. Treasury control is exercised as part of its general control over capital investment in the public sector and its responsibility for total government expenditure. Long-range forecasts of estimated expenditures, revenues, and capital must be submitted, as must be the ordinary estimates, and these forecasts provide the occasion for regular review and discussion with the authority of the financial implications of its policy.

These arrangements for co-ordinating and controlling the financial aspects of the authority's program appear to be satisfactory, but there is mounting criticism of the adequacy of the top structure for co-ordinating and balancing the various elements of the total scientific program of the nation.[5] Similar criticism has been directed at the possibly more apparent deficiencies in Canada, which shares the same type of cabinet and ministerial co-ordinating structure.

The minister for science not only has responsibilities other than atomic energy, he must also share those he has with other ministries such as Defence and the Armed Services. For the nuclear-power program, he must work especially with the minister

---

[5] See *Guardian* (Manchester), December 4, 1962, "Directing Research from the Top," for an outline of a report entitled "Science in Industry" which was prepared by the Conservative Political Center. This report especially criticized the top command for co-ordinating science: "The Government's scientific research and development effort should have a single decision-making point." The report called for a balancing of preferences "within the context of an overall view of national needs and resources."

of power. Indeed, the minister of power's responsibility for the nationalized electricity industry and his position as chief co-ordinator of national power policy as a whole force him, rather than the minister for science, to decide most of the arguments over the shares in the national power program which are to go to coal, oil, conventional electricity, and atomic power.[6]

The cabinet committee and a counterpart interdepartmental committee of permanent officials on nuclear-energy facilitate co-ordination and direction of the various aspects of the program. But there is a policy gap here created by the separation of these aspects; the minister for science lacks the jurisdictional authority to bridge the gap, and the co-ordinating committees lack the expertise to fill it. The co-ordination and control achieved through the Treasury's hold on the purse sets only outside limits to the program; what is decided within the liberal fiscal boundaries appears to be left to the "people who know" in the Atomic Energy Authority and its groups.

Canada. In addition to facing the same problems of co-ordination as the United States and Britain, Canada has to contend with two additional complications: (1) the heavy and direct involvement of the state in the production of source materials and (2) the existence of three specialized agencies sharing responsibility for separate portions of the program. To some extent the problem of co-ordination, especially of regulatory activities, is simplified when the government itself occupies a commanding position in all phases of the program; under these circumstances, regulation tends to become an internal problem. On the other hand, because the government's commitments are so great, the administrative burden has had to be divided among three agencies. Consequently, special care must be taken to ensure that the activities of each agency are properly co-ordinated.

The organizational solution to this problem was a statute conferring a formal primacy on one of the three agencies—the Atomic Energy Control Board. By serving as the central source of

---

[6] In 1960, when the nuclear power program was cut back in the face of a new crisis confronting Britain's nationalized coal industry, it was the minister of power who had the unpalatable task of announcing this.

regulations and by issuing all orders, licenses, and permits covering
every aspect of the program, the board obviously has the power
and is in the position to co-ordinate the entire program. In practice, the board has never played an operational role, but, with
its tiny secretariat, has contented itself with the policy questions
arising from its responsibility for promulgating regulations. Actual administration of the program is left to the other operating agencies—Eldorado Mining and Refining Ltd. and Atomic
Energy of Canada Ltd. Enforcement of the regulations is also in
the hands of such relevant departments as Health and Welfare
and Trade and Commerce.

Co-ordination of the three agencies is achieved partly by the
simple device of overlapping personnel: three of the five members on the board are drawn from the heads of the two operating
agencies and the National Research Council, which is the government's major scientific organization. In 1954, an amendment
to the act further rationalized the top co-ordinating mechanism
by making the board and its two operating agencies, as well as
the National Research Council, responsible to the minister who
is chairman of the Committee of the Privy Council on Scientific
Research.

This formal structure would appear to provide a coherent
framework for co-ordinating the activities of the separate atomic-
energy agencies and, at the same time, to permit the cabinet,
through its Scientific Research Committee, to assess the over-all
priorities in the nation's total scientific program. Closer examination reveals a less satisfactory state of affairs which gives rise
to the same criticisms that have been voiced in Britain. In recent years the cabinet committee has seldom met, and, in default
of any concerted consideration of the nation's entire scientific
effort, one must assume that each scientific establishment, including those responsible for atomic energy, has had to seek
through its own minister whatever funds it could convince the
Treasury Board to approve. In this respect the situation in Canada is less well co-ordinated than it is in England, for there, at
least, a minister for science does exist. In Canada, the minister
whose responsibilities for science as a whole derive from his position as chairman of a singularly inactive Committee could

scarcely be said to have the same status or comprehensive powers.[7]

In any event, the atomic-energy agencies do not appear to have suffered financial neglect because of the inadequacy of their representation in cabinet. This may be mainly attributed to the prestige and capabilities of the people who have been selected to preside over the activities of the agencies and the fact that this personal nexus of power is brought to a focus in the Atomic Energy Control Board, where each of them has a seat. Once again, one may legitimately question the effectiveness of lay controls over scientist-administrators.

Japan. Like Canada, Japan has elected to use several agencies rather than a single one for conducting its atomic-energy program; similar problems of co-ordination are therefore confronted. The organizational picture is, if anything, somewhat more complicated in Japan, but the administrative arrangements for resolving the problem of top-level co-ordination would appear to go much farther than those in Canada.

In Japan there are no fewer than six important bodies sharing responsibility for the nuclear-energy program. At the center of this organizational galaxy is the Atomic Energy Commission, the equivalent in power and status to Canada's Atomic Energy Control Board. The significant departure here is that this body is immediately under the prime minister. Responsibility for administering the entire atomic-energy program is conferred on the Science and Technics Agency, a body which also possesses more general surveillance over the entire scientific endeavor of the nation. In this agency, the Atomic Energy Bureau is responsible for the scientific and developmental aspects of nuclear energy. A unique combination of overlapping personnel and joint servicing arrangements appears to provide the maximum co-ordination. The director general of the Science and Technics Agency is the chairman of the Atomic Energy Commission; the Atomic Energy Bureau provides the secretariat for the commission. Under the bureau there is a third tier of agencies to whom

---

[7] For extended comment and criticism, see The Royal Commission on Government Organization, *Scientific Research and Development* (No. 23) (Ottawa: Queen's Printer, 1963), IV, 219–224.

operating roles have been assigned—research and development to the Atomic Energy Research Institute and the National Institute of Radiological Sciences, materials procurement and production to the Atomic Fuel Corporation.

The central position accorded the Atomic Energy Bureau is unique. The ganglia from this center of the nervous system reach upward to the Atomic Energy Commission, providing the technical signals which enable the commission to give the best information to the Prime Minister's Office. The ganglia reach downward and outward to the chief centers of operation, whether for the provision of raw and special materials or for commercial applications, research, or development.

The Atomic Energy Commission serves as the balance in this mechanism, consolidating the views of its own governmental organs with those coming from industry, the universities, local governments, and the general scientific community. The bureau's close relation with the commission has strengthened its co-ordinating powers when dealing with the subordinate nuclear-energy agencies and with ministries whose fields of operation cut across the atomic energy program.

Reinforcing this co-ordinating machinery are two other devices. The first is the familiar regular budgetary process on which other countries, particularly the United States and the United Kingdom, have placed such reliance. Before being sent to the minister of finance, all the estimates for each aspect of the nuclear-energy program are reviewed and revised by the Atomic Energy Commission. The larger portion of these, concerned with research and development, is consolidated in the estimates for the Atomic Energy Bureau and, when the Diet has approved it, is redistributed to the operating agencies.

These budgetary reviews are undertaken within the framework of the second, and unusual, co-ordinating device—the Long Range Program. This program was provisionally established by the commission at the outset in 1956. But in February, 1961, a more ambitious plan was published, outlining two ten-year periods, the first characterized by a program leading to scientific and technological self-sufficiency, the second by the full flowering of commercial utilization. Since public funds are expected to play the predominant role in the first stage, the commission has a yardstick for establishing the direction and priorities of the specific activities making up the program. Some ten or more special committees, most of them *ad hoc,* enlist the help of outside and governmental experts in assessing the policies and programs to be pursued under the plan.

Altogether, Japan appears to have developed ingenious and effective devices for ensuring that the numerous agencies participating in separate aspects of the atomic-energy program are working together. The vital policy decisions reach the prime minister through the Atomic Energy Commission, and the formal means of enlisting maximum expert advice in the formulation of policy appear to be equally well in hand. The greatest trial of the efficacy of the co-ordinating mechanism will come with the inevitable enlargement of the state's activities in implementing the promises of the first ten years' of Japan's Long Range Program.

France. France faces precisely the same problems of co-ordination as the countries already discussed, and its co-ordinating mechanisms are not altogether dissimilar. Like most other countries, the budgetary process has been used as the primary mechanism, and like Japan France has used formal long-range plans to buttress the budgetary review.

The concentration in one agency of the major activities associated with the peaceful uses of atomic energy avoids some of the co-ordinating problems which have faced both Canada and Japan. Nevertheless, in the regulatory field and in the commercial application of nuclear energy, the operations of the Atomic Energy Authority overlap, as they do elsewhere, the traditional jurisdictions of long-established departments.

Co-ordination of the many-sided operations of the commission is achieved by means of a somewhat unusual double-barreled arrangement: a general manager (*administrateur général délégué du gouvernement*) who is in charge of finance and administration and a high commissioner (*haut commissaire*) who is responsible for directing the authority's scientific and technical work. Presiding over these two officials is the eleven-man governing board (Comité de l'Énergie Atomique) of which the chairman is the prime minister (although he can designate a ministerial alternate in whose absence the general manager presides). It is interesting to note that the make-up of the board follows a pattern set elsewhere in that it gives representation to those with major administrative responsibilities in nuclear and related fields. Thus, both the general manager and the high commissioner are on the board, along with the directors of the French Electricity Authority and the National Center for Scientific Research, the Budget director, a representative of the armed service, and a university representative.

France, like the United States and Japan, has taken special precautions to place final responsibility for co-ordination and larger policy decisions in the hands of the chief political executive officer, the prime minister. The fact that other departments may conflict with the Atomic Energy Authority in exercising their traditional prerogatives over health, labor, safety, housing, trade, and industry, no doubt accounts for this arrangement. In this process the budget is employed as the final arbiter. Five-year plans, approved by the legislature, are used as the bases for making the annual budgetary allocations, and there has been a progressive systematization and expansion of the details in these budgets, which reflect the effort to achieve closer control. A rapidly increasing proportion of the authority's revenues comes from the Fund for Economic and Social Development, so that the investment in the scientific and developmental program of the authority is assessed in the light of the broader considerations affecting the nation's total expenditures for social utilities of all kinds.

Italy. Earlier references to the still-unsettled organization for administering Italy's atomic-energy program suggest that the problem of co-ordination will be exceptionally acute. At the moment, the minister of industry and commerce is clearly the dominant co-ordinating force in the system. He is not only a member of the ministerial committee which lays down the general policy and programs, but he is also chairman of the National Committee for Nuclear Energy. In addition, as the minister who is answerable to the legislature for the operations of the National Committee, he is placed in the distinctly ambiguous position of sitting in judgment on himself. This dual role will undoubtedly create future legal or political problems, and it would seem that the most logical way of clarifying the situation would be to follow other countries in making the committee directly responsible to the prime minister.

The problem of achieving co-operation among the National Committee and the numerous other ministries having some share or interest in the regulatory and operative aspects of the nuclear-energy program is partly solved by the device used in other countries—the management board which really conducts the affairs of the National Committee for Nuclear Energy includes among its expert and technical members the directors general of the Ministry of Industry and Commerce and of the Ministry of Public Education. Similarly, the ministerial committee which determines policy includes, in addition to the prime minister himself, the home minister, the ministers of foreign affairs, the Treasury, industry and commerce, and education; other interested ministers may participate as the occasion demands.

The program in Italy, compared with the other countries under review, is less developed, and although one can observe the same co-ordinating problems emerging, the need for more formal co-ordinating machinery is not quite so imperative at this stage.

Co-ordination of International Activities. The proliferation of international organizations devoted to the peaceful uses of atomic energy occasions much the same necessity for devising effective co-ordinating mechanisms as has proliferation at the national level. In a sense, these international organizations may be loosely compared to their national counterparts: the General Assembly of the United Nations is the parliament; the International Atomic Energy Agency is the equivalent of a national atomic-energy authority; the World Health Organization is a ministry of health; the European Nuclear Energy Authority is a regional nuclear-energy conference comparable, for example, with the Nuclear Energy Conference of the Southern states in the United

ADMINISTERING THE ATOM FOR PEACE

States; international research institutes have their domestic parallel in such establishments as the Associated Universities that operate the Brookhaven Laboratory in the United States; and so on. But the analogy breaks down when it is recognized that at the international level there is no single central authority capable of assigning to all the relevant organizations complementary functions. Consequently, the mechanisms devised to achieve co-ordination of international efforts have several unique features.

One of these devices, the relationship agreement, is simply a formal way of setting out the respective jurisdictions of the parties to the agreement. This formality is required because sovereign states are dealing with one another. Although it is sometimes true that a department in one state must often feel that in its dealings with other departments it might just as well be negotiating with a foreign power, usually the understandings reached are not expressed in formal treaties, and there is presumably a higher authority to act as final adjudicator.

The most important relationship agreement in the nuclear-energy field is that between the United Nations and the International Atomic Energy Agency, concluded immediately after the agency came into being. The agreement establishes the primacy of the IAEA in the United Nations with respect to nuclear energy; it obligates the agency to make regular reports to the General Assembly, the Security Council, and the Economic and Social Council and also provides for IAEA's co-operation with various scientific and administrative bodies sponsored by the United Nations.

Agreements have also been used to confirm the relationships between the agency and seven of the specialized agencies of the United Nations, such as the World Health Organization, UNESCO, and the International Labour Organization. In addition to delimiting the spheres of action of each agency, the agreements provide for representation of the agencies at each of the other's principal meetings or conferences. Consultation on matters of joint interest and provision for shared efforts are also envisaged. Pursuant to these agreements, the IAEA will, for example, consult with WHO before entering any research contracts providing for the medical use of radioisotopes or with the Food and Agriculture Organization before giving technical assistance or concluding research contracts involving agriculture. Joint conferences have frequently been arranged, culminating in the issuance of joint publications.

Regional nuclear-energy organizations have entered similar relationship agreements with the International Atomic Energy Agency, although these have been much less specific because both parties are concerned primarily, rather than peripherally (as are the other specialized agencies), with nuclear energy.

A variation on these formal agreements is used when it is desirable to establish relations with non-governmental organizations. For this purpose, following a pattern generally employed by the United Nations, a grant of consultative status is conferred, entitling these organizations to receive information from the IAEA on its activities, as well as to attend certain meetings or submit information to the secretariat and other organs of the agency. By these means, some of the non-governmental organizations, notably the International Commission on Radiological Protection, have participated vigorously in certain activities of the agency.

Although relationship agreements provide the formal bases for interagency co-ordination, means must be found to reconcile conflicts and generally to police the agreements. Obviously, this requires the interposition of higher authorities than the specialized agencies. For the United Nations agencies, the principal co-ordinating power is vested in the Economic and Social Council. All specialized agencies—including the International Atomic Energy Agency—must make annual reports to the council, which is charged by the Charter of the United Nations and by the General Assembly with the task of co-ordinating their work. The council accomplishes this task by analyzing the programs of all the agencies, by convening conferences to thrash out problems, by formally assigning certain areas of work to one organization and requesting others to co-operate, and through preparing long-term plans in which the work of all the organizations is integrated.[8]

---

[8] The most ambitious of these is a five-year study, covering 1960–1965, of the work of the various United Nations organs and related agencies in the economic and social fields.

Another top-level co-ordinating organ is the Administrative Committee for Co-ordination, which consists of the executive heads of the various agencies and is presided over by the secretary-general of the United Nations. At periodic meetings of this committee and of certain subcommittees (including one on the peaceful uses of atomic energy), recommendations for co-ordinating action are formulated and passed to the relevant special agency or to the parent body, ECOSOC.

As in each country, the budget is also a useful device for co-ordination. The Advisory Committee on Administrative and Budgetary Questions, which examines and reports on the budgets of bodies like the International Atomic Energy Agency, helps call to the attention of the General Assembly any overlapping programs. A major portion of the money granted to the IAEA comes from two United Nations funds for technical assistance —the Expanded Program of Technical Assistance and the Special Fund. Special organs reporting to the Economic and Social Council control the application of these funds and consequently provide a means of integrating all programs for assisting underdeveloped states.

The ultimate guarantors of a proper division of responsibilities are, of course, the national governments of the various participants. Some assurance that there will be no conscious duplication is provided in the network of national memberships in the same organizations—thus, for example, membership on the International Atomic Energy Agency is substantially identical to membership on the United Nations specialized agencies; all members of EURATOM are in the European Nuclear Energy Agency, whose members, in turn, are all on the IAEA. It may be presumed, under these circumstances, that, if, for example, the IAEA is assigned a particular piece of work, the same member states in the World Health Organization are not likely to ask WHO to perform the same task. Admittedly this cross-membership is not foolproof, for, particularly when it comes to the detailed development of a program by the secretariat of an organization, there may be opportunities for duplication. Where memberships do not coincide, of course, these chances are enlarged. And even where membership coincides, representatives of the same government may have conflicting views as to the desirable division of work. This could happen, for example, if the representatives on the Board of the International Atomic Energy Agency received instructions from the national atomic-energy commissions that conflicted with the directions given, for example, to the respective ministries of agriculture represented on the Food and Agriculture Organization Conference.

Finally, it is interesting to observe that at the international level, just as in each nation, the use of the same persons on different organizations provides an informal but effective co-ordinating force. There are many instances of this: the same persons appear on the Scientific Advisory Committee of the United Nations and of the International Atomic Energy Agency; overlapping personnel are also common on the technical advisory committees responsible for jointly operated regional scientific establishments like EUROCHEMIC, DRAGON, and HALDEN. This development is probably attributable less to deliberate policy than to the scarcity of qualified specialists in nuclear energy.

Conclusions. Not unexpectedly, the co-ordination devices employed by various countries are adapted to the peculiar governmental structures of each. Nevertheless, there is a surprising uniformity in the methods used. Common to all, including the international organizations, is the pervasive and overriding use of the general budget to ensure that the atomic-energy program is properly balanced against other elements of the nation's scientific effort. In several countries this general surveillance has been reinforced by bringing the chief executive officer—president or prime minister—directly into all major policy decisions. The success with which he performs his role of arbitrator and decision-maker depends on a proper mechanism for co-ordinating the flow of expert advice on which he must base his judgments. In several countries it is concluded that this area of co-ordination has been the least satisfactory, for it raises a problem of expert-to-layman relations which has long been regarded as critical in the realm of military-civil relations; with the great advances in science and technology, these have now assumed broader and more pervasive dimensions.

At the working level, as distinct from the policy level, the device of interagency co-ordinating committees is found in all countries. This procedure is extended at the international level by formal agreements, but even in each country—in the United States, for example—a species of "treaty" between the agencies concerned with special aspects of the nuclear-energy program (especially where federal-state jurisdiction is involved) can be said to exist. Judicious cross-fertilization of agencies with key personnel from the participating organs is an almost universal practice, for the same people repeatedly appear, wearing different hats as members of the governing boards of the various atomic-energy bodies. Although this procedure has obvious merits in fostering co-ordination and may be a necessary consequence of the limited number of people with the requisite scientific knowledge, it has, nevertheless, all the earmarks of a new type of family compact the implications of which are examined in the next chapter.

VIII
Accountability

Throughout this study, frequent reference has been made to the problem of establishing the ultimate accountability of the agencies charged with administering the atomic-energy program. The problem is essentially twofold: first, in setting up specialized atomic-energy authorities outside the conventional system of departments, how to maintain the normal controlling functions of the executive and the legislature; second, the more subtle problem, how to preserve the traditional authority of politically responsible laymen over the scientist-administrator.

Executive and Legislative Controls. In general, it is clear that the selection of such non-departmental forms of organization as commissions, authorities, public corporations, Crown companies, and mixed enterprises is by no means confined to administering the atomic-energy program. The problems of preserving accountability to the executive and legislative branches are, therefore, familiar to all practitioners and students of government, who were concerned with the consequences of an almost universal proliferation of non-departmental administration long before the advent of nuclear energy.

Atomic energy meets most of the classical rationalizations that have been developed in many countries to sustain the departure from the traditional form. The field is very new and expanding rapidly in directions which cannot be clearly foreseen at the outset. Hence, flexibility is of the essence—flexibility to manage skilled manpower and the large investments in plant and equipment which are characteristic of atomic-energy programs. Many of the activities are akin to private industrial undertakings and must work closely with private concerns—hence, the need to devise board-management relations that are molded more to the pattern of private enterprise than to the rigid hierarchy of the civil service. In addition, most of the trading in raw materials and finished products is on an intergovernmental basis, thus lending more weight to the claim for separate specialized agencies. Finally, the dual character of the program—actually or potentially applicable to both war and peace—together with its vast dimensions and the uniquely hazardous nature of its substances and processes, supports the argument for special agencies rather than a number of existing departments.

Because much has already been said about the mechanics of exercising executive and legislative control over the specialized agencies, here it is necessary only to provide a summary of the main elements.

Executive control is exerted in a number of ways. The power to appoint and to discharge members of the commission or the governing board is universally conferred on the executive—the president, the prime minister or another responsible minister answerable for the authority in the legislature, or by the collegial action of the cabinet (a customary provision in Canada, for example). Beyond this initial, though critical, point the ancient dictum of Lord Macaulay "to choose wisely and to confide liberally" appears to be much in evidence—with the important exception of the United States. In its practical application, the dictum is expressed as a grant of authority to the directing heads of the agency to manage day-to-day affairs without detailed intervention by the executive.

Executive control over the broader policy decisions of the atomic-energy agencies is maintained by a variety of means. In the United States, for example, the president alone is empowered to make the final determinations concerning the quantities of fissionable materials to be produced and the export quotas to foreign powers with whom the United States has agreements. Canada and the United Kingdom handle this problem in a different way, by conferring on their atomic-energy agencies a virtual monopoly over source and special nuclear materials. In their use of these monopolistic powers, the governing boards are subject in Britain to both specific and general directions issued by the responsible minister and in Canada to cabinet approval of contracts and regulations made by the atomic-energy agencies. In France and Italy, the bridge between the executive and the special authorities is established by placing cabinet ministers on the policy boards. In Japan, the prime minister, though not a member of the boards, must confirm many of the decisions—often in considerable detail—taken by the Atomic Energy Commission and its operating satellites.

The programs of the atomic-energy authorities are also controlled by the annual executive review of budgets. In all countries, this review is much more like that to which a regular department is subjected than that imposed on other industrial undertakings of the government, for none of these agencies is capable of financing from operating revenues more than ten per cent of its total program. This has meant that the executive considers and approves not only capital programs, but also the operating budgets of the several nuclear-energy bodies.

Finally the atomic-energy program impinges on the activities of many other departments and agencies. In the process of co-ordinating these agencies at the executive level, any tendency on the part of the specialized atomic-energy authorities to make unilateral decisions is offset by the need to accommodate the views and claims of the related agencies. There are numerous devices for achieving this co-ordination, none of which is wholly satisfactory, although each has the objective of ensuring that the atomic-energy program is kept in balance with the government's endeavors in related fields.

Legislative controls over atomic-energy agencies are probably no more and no less satisfactory than those which have been established over other non-departmental forms of organization. All agencies, to begin with, are statutory creations. The legislature of each country has, in fact, tended to prescribe in unusual detail the powers to be devolved on the atomic-energy authorities and the manner in which the powers are to be exercised. The Japanese Diet has, perhaps, gone the furthest in circumscribing the discretion of the atomic-energy agencies through numerous, detailed enactments. Atomic energy, however, has not been singled out for special treatment; since the war and the Occupation, a characteristic feature of law-making has been the effort "to prevent the resurgence of the system, under which a wide range of executive-issued orders and decrees . . . had the force of law and could be issued at the discretion of the all-powerful executive without approval or, in many cases, even challenge by the Imperial Diet." [1]

The legislature's effort to exert control by detailed enactments is limited by the unknown nature of atomic energy, which makes it difficult to evolve detailed prescriptions in advance. In fact, the most fruitful contribution of the legislative branch is to be found in its largely ex post facto scrutiny of the atomic-energy agencies. The tabling of annual reports of these bodies in the legislature may provide the occasion for general debate on policies and programs, although the evidence is that none of the countries surveyed actually takes much advantage of this opportunity. Much more reliance is placed on legislative committees. The committee device in Japan, for example, was used to good effect in the formative stages of the atomic-energy program. A ten-member bipartisan Joint Committee on Atomic Energy was extremely active between 1954 and 1958 in shaping the basic atomic-energy law and the detailed enactments subsequently required to give it flesh and blood. After 1958, partisan differences split the committee and destroyed its influence, although wide press and television coverage of all Diet committee proceedings still focuses critical public attention on their work.

In France, legislative attention has been directed much more to the military side of the atomic-energy program, where the keenest debates have surrounded the country's efforts to build its own nuclear striking force. The necessity of securing legislative approval for successive five-year plans provides sporadic opportunity for a global review of the program, but such reviews have tended to be perfunctory. The atomic-energy budget must go through the regular financial control commission channels

---

[1] John M. Maki, *Government and Politics in Japan* (London: Thames and Hudson, 1962), p. 94.

of the legislature, and it may also be placed before one of the six standing commissions to which the Chamber was reduced at the beginning of the Fifth Republic. Neither of these appears to be supported by the necessary technical advice which might render it more effective. In fact, there has never been any suggestion that a special legislative committee on atomic energy might be desirable.[2]

In the United Kingdom, the program of the authority can be, and in 1959 actually was, examined in detail by the Select Committee on Estimates. Similarly, the Public Accounts Committee is also empowered to scrutinize the accounts of the authority.[3] Both committees report to the House of Commons, and, although each may suppress information on security grounds, neither has been prevented from securing secret information even though it cannot be publicized or publicly debated. The reports of these two committees, as well as the annual report of the authority itself, may be the subject of a full-dress debate in the House. On the whole, the legislature is not placed at a disadvantage in discussing atomic-energy matters—no more than it is, say, in exercising its control over defense production or foreign affairs. This is to admit, however, that legislative surveillance in this area, as in the field of public corporations generally, is far from satisfactory.

Legislative control in Canada has normally been exercised even more sporadically than in the United Kingdom. The device of special Parliamentary committees has been used, roughly at two- to three-year intervals, to review all the government's research activities, always with particular attention to atomic-energy matters because of the intense activity and high costs involved. The committee proceedings have been characterized by

---

[2] *Le Monde* (Paris), January 10, 1963, reported that Gaston Palewski, minister of state for scientific research, space, and atomic-energy matters, had set up a new financial committee for the French Atomic Energy Authority, but this would appear to be part of the machinery for executive rather than legislative control and is designed particularly to ease the tasks of the governing board of the authority in assessing the annual budget (particularly contracts). The board had apparently become incapable of grappling with a budget that had risen from 760,000,000 fr. in 1958 to 3,000,000,000 fr. in 1963.

[3] The authority, however, falls outside the scope of the Select Committee on Nationalized Industries.

efficient presentation on the part of the respective government agencies, but one has the impression that, apart from the salutary educational service rendered the members, officials actually use the opportunity to obtain a rather uncritical stamp of approval for the results of their stewardship. Occasionally, the committee has offered a public platform from which the very few outside, independent experts could criticize the program, but to argue that this is realistic control over the pace and direction of the atomic-energy program would be to greatly exaggerate the modest role played by these committees.

A much different picture of legislative control emerges in the United States. The Joint Congressional Committee on Atomic Energy is by all odds more influential than any of the legislative controls adopted in the other countries in this survey. Indeed, it is not only unique with respect to other countries; it also has no counterpart among the many committees which constitute such an essential part of the United States government. It is the only permanent joint committee that has ever been established in the Congress and that has continuing responsibility for directly recommending legislation to the House and Senate.[4] The association of what is essentially a unicameral working unit with an otherwise completely bicameral legislature has had the effect of strengthening Congress in its dealings with the executive branch. As Green and Rosenthal, have aptly summed up this relationship: "In the field of atomic energy, Congress, or at least its surrogate committee, acts with distinctive vigor and notable success as watchdog, gadfly, partner, and policy-maker." [5]

The history of this relationship illuminates the positive contribution of the Joint Committee even as it raises a general question concerning its applicability to other areas of administration. At the outset, the committee was passive, presumably accumulating the necessary knowledge about the new energy source. By 1954, it was actively initiating legislative amendments, demanding to be informed *before* decisions had been taken, and requiring certain policy decisions to lie before it for thirty days before

---

[4] The uniqueness of this committee has naturally attracted much attention. See, for example, Morgan Thomas, *Atomic Energy and Congress* (Ann Arbor: University of Michigan Press, 1956), and Green and Rosenthal, *op. cit.,* on which this text relies for its comments.

[5] *Ibid.,* p. i.

they were acted on. Subsequently, the committee used its power to authorize appropriations for plant construction and acquisition of real property to accelerate the pace of the domestic reactor program, sometimes, as in 1958, to encourage a development which did not have the enthusiastic support of the executive branch. Over the years, the membership of the committee has tended to remain fairly stable, and the members have conscientiously sought to master the mysteries of the atomic-energy program. As long as the committee remains united, it carries great weight on the floor of the House. The increasing sophistication of its members, a strong staff, and its statutory claim over "all bills, resolutions, and other matters . . . relating primarily to the Commission or to the development, use, or control of atomic energy" have enabled the Joint Committee to pre-empt the role of leader which the Atomic Energy Commission might have been expected to assert. Its claims to power have even extended to overriding both the AEC and the Bureau of the Budget in the item-by-item review of the budget or in adding funds against the wishes of these two agencies.

It is not suggested that this legislative device could be adapted to the legislative controls of other countries; it is, after all, unique in its own country. The Atomic Energy Commission and its isolation from effective presidential control and support have no parallel. The Joint Committee, in a sense, has stepped into the policy gap between the chief executive and the Atomic Energy Commission.

> By 1955, the Committee had become an aggressive claimant for the right to participate on an equal basis in the formulation of atomic-energy policy. Finally, during the latter years of the Eisenhower administration and into the first years of the Kennedy presidency, the Committee's decisive influence was fully recognized and accepted by the executive branch. . . . [A]ccrued influence and habits of leadership ensure that it will continue to play an important role in atomic-energy policy-making.[6]

Green and Rosenthal conclude: "The JCAE exerts its influence largely through continuous participation in the Executive's deliberations, rather than by legislating." [7] Other countries are

---

[6] *Ibid.*, p. 20.
[7] *Ibid.*, p. 268.

bound to examine this rare specimen with curiosity—perhaps with envy—but they are not likely to be in a position to emulate it.

Apart from this spectacular exception in the United States, the relations between atomic-energy authorities and the agencies of legislative and executive control differ little from those that have developed for similar non-departmental forms. Whatever is unusual about the problem of accountability, then, derives from the expert-to-layman relationship.

The Expert's Accountability to the Layman. Thus far, attention has been directed to the availability and effectiveness of the instruments by which politically responsible officials exercise control. On the whole, the adequacy of control mechanisms gives no greater cause for concern than it does for other complex state undertakings; more alarming are the issues posed when inquiring into the conditions under which control is exercised and into the consequences for the experts who must be subjected to such controls.

Perhaps the two most important controlling mechanisms derive from the power over the budget and the power to make regulations. It is through the budget that operating priorities of the atomic-energy program are established. But priorities involve choices, and the critical question is whether national budget-makers, as lay politicians and administrators, can really make informed choices when they consider the complex operating programs in the field of atomic energy. Similarly, the power to make the regulations which govern the way in which nuclear energy will be deployed in the community at large assumes that the politically responsible layman has a complete grasp of the scientific and technical components which the regulations must embrace. The promulgation of such regulations cannot be left to the experts, for in most cases technical considerations constitute only one set of factors relevant to the final decision. For this reason, major regulations are promulgated in all countries by the highest politically responsible officials, who are guided but should not be dominated by the expert advisors.

In the context of the democratic state, those who use the

levers of control are accountable to the people. If this accountability is to be meaningful, there must be a public with sufficient knowledge of and perception about atomic-energy matters
to carry on an informed public dialogue with the policy-makers.
Thus, the political officials must be responsive to the public, and
the public must have positive views to which the policy-makers
can respond. In the absence of an informed, attentive public,
politicians are apt to become passive, thereby creating a policy
vacuum into which the committed expert with strong views can
readily move and guide the subsequent course of events. Sir
Charles Snow has recently characterized this situation as a system
of "closed politics," which he describes as "any kind of politics
in which there is no appeal to a larger assembly—larger assembly
in the sense of a group of opinions, or an electorate, or on an
even bigger scale what we call loosely 'social forces.' " [8] Where
these conditions prevail, he observes, there is an opportunity for
the scientist-statesman or the scientist-administrator to gain immense behind-the-scenes power over the politically responsible
laymen.

The safeguard against pre-emption of power by politically ir-
responsible experts is the existence of countervailing sources of
influence. No expert should be placed in a position where he
alone has access to the highest political authority. The answer,
then, seems to lie in achieving the most appropriate balance of the
views of various experts and, indeed, a superficial inspection of
the situation in the United States, for example, suggests that this
is precisely what has been done. Free competition among a variety
of experts located at a number of strategic points of access to the
president prevents domination by a "science czar" and permits a
viable compromise on the range of choices offered to the chief
executive.[9]

The foregoing comments are not intended as a formulation
of a new conspiracy theory, the product of a dark and deliberate

---

[8] C. P. Snow, *Science and Government* (Cambridge, Mass.: Harvard University Press, 1961), p. 56.

[9] "The plurality of this process is important for the preservation of the
health and vitality of science itself," according to Jerome B. Wiesner, director of the Office of Science and Technology, quoted in *Bulletin of the
Atomic Scientists*, XVIII (November 1962), 45.

design on the part of the technocrats to replace the politically responsible layman in the scheme of things. The scientist, whether he likes it or not, is being dragged into the scientifically-oriented twentieth century, there to occupy an increasingly important place in decision-making. Prof. Warner R. Schilling has recently identified this development and the considerations that should guide it:

> The scientist, in short, is not likely to orbit the centers of political power emitting upon request "beeps" of purely technical information. He will inevitably be pulled into the political arena. If his participation there is to be either productive or personally satisfying, both the scientist and the non-scientist need to be highly conscious of the character of their activity and the problems involved. The scientist (and many a non-scientist) must learn that the making of . . . policy is not a quest for the "right" answers to the problems of our time. There are only hard choices, the consequences of which will be uncertain and the making of which will often seem interminable in time and irrational in procedure.
>
> The debate and disagreement over these choices will be heated and confused under the best of circumstances, but emotion and misunderstanding can be eased if scientists and non-scientists are both alert to the limits as well as the potential of the scientist's contribution. On the scientist's part, there is the obvious need to exercise the utmost care in making clear to himself and to others the areas where he speaks as a concerned citizen and those where he speaks as a professional expert. More difficult will be the task of learning how and to whom to address himself in each of these capacities when he is dissatisfied with the outcome of a policy decision in which he has participated.[10]

Professor Schilling's comments apply with particular force to the exceptionally "open" political processes in the United States, but they are generally relevant for any democratic society.

The problem of expert-to-amateur relationships is only partly met by creating conditions wherein the countervailing opinions of many experts establish the norms of public policy; policy decisions have to be based not merely on scientific factors, but also on social and economic considerations. For these the policy-makers must ultimately fall back on the general public,

---

[10] Warner R. Schilling, "Scientists, Foreign Policy, and Politics," *American Political Science Review*, LVI (June 1962), 298–299. A similar point, with illustrations, is made throughout the equally fine analysis by Don K. Price, *op. cit.*

and, as has been suggested, on questions concerning atomic energy, the policy-makers are likely to meet with an inattentive and ill-informed public.

The conditions in which atomic energy was born have contributed to this situation. Secrecy characterized every aspect of its early development; costs, though stupendous, were irrelevant when national security was at stake, and the general public sat back in fear as it watched the mushroom cloud spread. The emergency is still not altogether over, but much of the secrecy is no longer necessary, and growing public familiarity with nuclear energy breeds puzzled apathy if not contempt. The scientist and the engineer still preside over a house of mysteries which, for all its potential good, is still beyond the critical comprehension of the public at large. At the same time, all skills and knowledge in this esoteric area tend to be sucked into the government's establishments or at least are so closely identified with them through contractual relations with a few large private enterprises that there remain few genuinely independent centers of intellectually respectable criticism.

Decision-making in the field of atomic energy is attended by the same hazards that have been so prominently identified with the procurement of weapons systems. The costs of pursuing one line of development in reactor technology, for example, are such that only a few of the wealthiest and most technically advanced nations can afford a diversified program which permits them to abandon the least promising projects. All the eggs tend to be placed in one type of nuclear-reactor basket, largely on the strength of the scientific experts' judgment. If subsequent developments elsewhere prove that the wrong basket has been selected, professional pride and the almost overwhelming costs of making a change will provide natural justifications for the scientific fraternity to close ranks and reaffirm the courage and correctness of their convictions. The rare critic who dares to protest is met with that patient but supremely confident reassurance which somehow exposes him as a person with an ax to grind or as an obvious crank.[11]

---

[11] Just such a situation occurred recently in Canada, for example, when an expert critic challenged the government scientists' commitment to the natural uranium, heavy-water–reactor technology on which the whole program

Maintaining a program for the peaceful applications of nuclear energy involves an enormous commitment on the part of the government—a commitment of money, staff, and plant that is based essentially on little more than the experts' informed guess on the "best" projects to pursue. Programs of such dimensions tend to build up a momentum of their own, which discourages drastic revisions. The momentum can be checked or redirected only if politicians are prepared to face the unpalatable task of assuming their responsibility to the people for having accepted expert advice which time may have proved to be wrong.

The prospect of a political system dominated by technocrats has, no doubt, been unduly exaggerated in attempting to identify the important issues raised when seeking to preserve the conventional system of lay controls over the expert. There are obviously great, almost infinite, possibilities awaiting the peaceful applications of atomic energy in such fields as medicine, agriculture, industry, power development, and transportation. A concern for the administrative problems encountered in developing this new source of energy should not be regarded as a valid reason for decrying the obvious benefits to be derived from its fullest exploitation. Nevertheless, as a final cautionary note, it may be argued that, in the first flush of enthusiasm and in the absence of informed lay judgment to keep this enthusiasm in proper proportion, most nations may have deployed too much of their effort in this field. "Keeping up with the Jones's" is as natural an instinct among nations as among individuals, particularly when, as in the early stages of atomic-energy development, this was literally a life-and-death matter. Has it not now developed into an overly expensive patriotic fad, encouraged by dedicated scientists who had no difficulty in infecting laymen with their enthusiasm for the brave new nuclear world? The time may indeed have arrived for a much more hardheaded reappraisal of the relation between costs and expected returns in dollars and in human well-being.

---

had been based since the war years, when Canada's assignment was to explore and develop this line of research. See Peter C. Newman, "The Field of Atomic Power: two experts meet," *Maclean's Magazine*, July 29, 1961, p. 48.

Index